THE LIBRARIAN, THE SCHOLAR, AND THE FUTURE OF THE RESEARCH LIBRARY

Recent Titles in
Contributions in Librarianship and Information Science

The Politics of an Emerging Profession: The American Library Association, 1876-1917
Wayne A. Wiegand

Foreign Students in American Library Education: Impact on Home Countries
Maxine K. Rochester

Academic Librarians and Cataloging Networks: Visibility, Quality Control, and Professional Status
Ruth Hafter

Activism in American Librarianship, 1962-1973
Mary Lee Bundy and Frederick J. Stielow, editors

Librarianship: A Third World Perspective
Rosario Gassol de Horowitz

Pascal Programming for Libraries: Illustrative Examples for Information Specialists
Charles H. Davis, Gerald W. Lundeen, and Debora Shaw

The Culture and Control of Expertise: Toward a Sociological Understanding of Librarianship
Michael F. Winter

The American Public Library and the Problem of Purpose
Patrick Williams

Public Librarianship: An Issues-Oriented Approach
Verna L. Pungitore

Naturalistic Inquiry for Library Science: Methods and Applications for Research, Evaluation, and Teaching
Constance Ann Mellon

From Documentation to Information Science: The Beginnings and Early Development of the American Documentation Institute—American Society for Information Science
Irene S. Farkas-Conn

The Decision-Making Process for Library Collections: Case Studies in Four Types of Libraries
Beatrice Kovacs

The Librarian, the Scholar, and the Future of the Research Library

Eldred Smith

CONTRIBUTIONS IN LIBRARIANSHIP AND INFORMATION SCIENCE, NUMBER 66

Paul Wasserman, *Series Editor*

GREENWOOD PRESS
New York • Westport, Connecticut • London

Library of Congress Cataloging-in-Publication Data

Smith, Eldred R.
    The librarian, the scholar, and the future of the research library / Eldred Smith.
        p. cm.—(Contributions in librarianship and information science, ISSN 0084-9243 ; no. 66)
    Includes bibliographical references.
    ISBN 0-313-27210-7 (lib. bdg. : alk. paper)
    1. Research libraries. 2. Libraries and scholars. 3. Library science—Forecasting. 4. Library science—Technological innovations. 5. Research—Technological innovations. 6. Information technology. I. Title. II. Series.
Z675.R45S6 1990
027.7—dc20   89-25665

British Library Cataloguing in Publication Data is available.

Copyright © 1990 by Eldred Smith

All rights reserved. No portion of this book may be reproduced, by any process or technique, without the express written consent of the publisher.

Library of Congress Catalog Card Number: 89-25665
ISBN: 0-313-27210-7
ISSN: 0084-9243

First published in 1990

Greenwood Press, 88 Post Road West, Westport, Connecticut 06881
An imprint of Greenwood Publishing Group, Inc.

Printed in the United States of America

∞

The paper used in this book complies with the Permanent Paper Standard issued by the National Information Standards Organization (Z39.48-1984).

10 9 8 7 6 5 4 3 2 1

For Judy

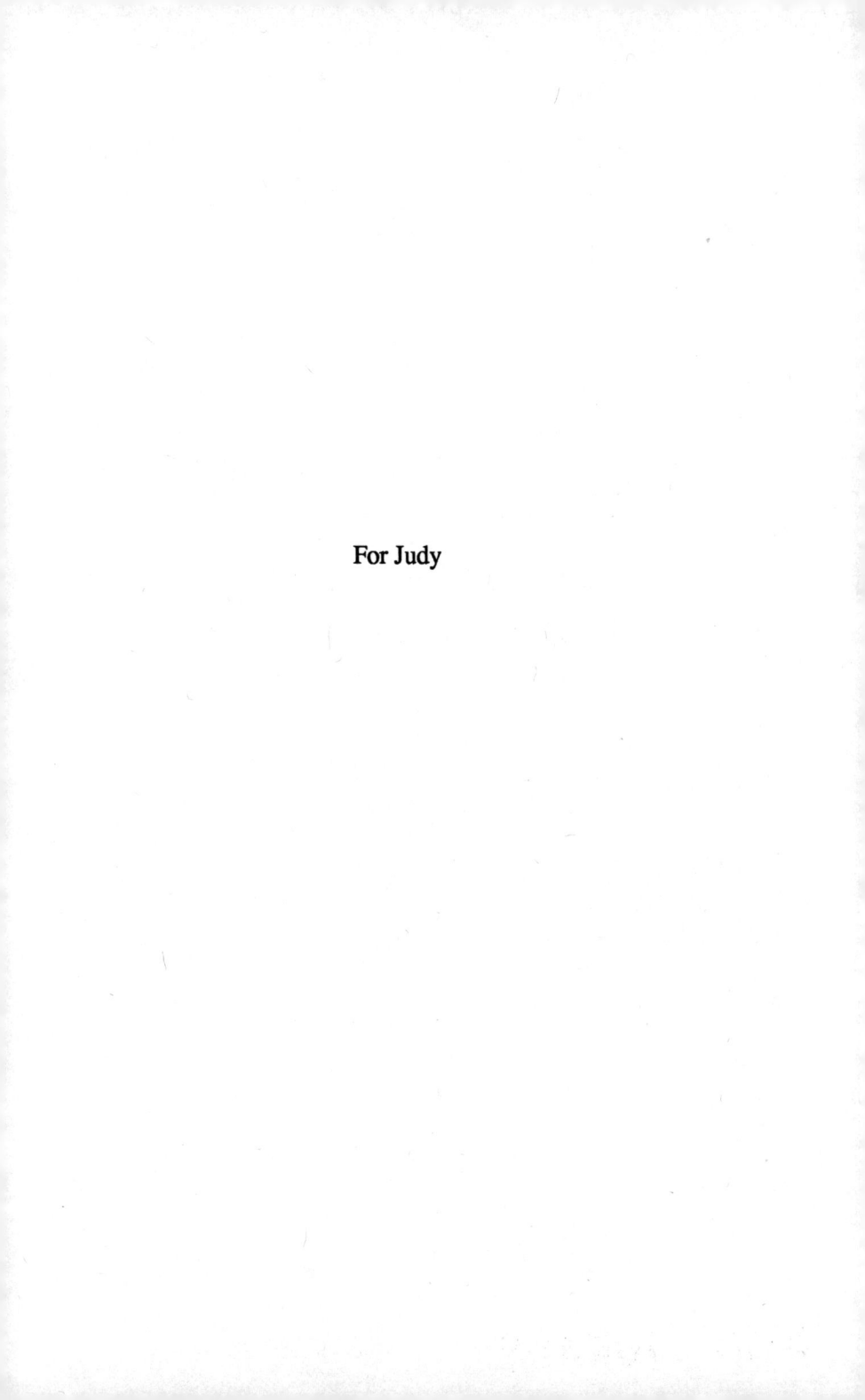

But this complex of cultural conditions may well evoke a vision of the future librarian as a knowledgeable sluicekeeper, a most sensitive filter, a wise *cicerone* who knows where what knowledge is available, how to get its essential parts, someone who does not block access but also someone who does not drown us in an unsorted morass of information.

Karl. A. Weintraub

Contents

Introduction	1
1. The Librarian and Information	5
2. The Scholar and Information	17
3. The Influence of Technology	29
4. From Cooperation to Collaboration	41
5. Directing Change	55
6. Controlled Completeness: Consolidating the Record of Scholarship	65
7. Reliable Convenience: The Future Research Library	77
Bibliographic Essay	87
Index	117

THE LIBRARIAN, THE SCHOLAR, AND THE FUTURE OF THE RESEARCH LIBRARY

Introduction

Today's research librarian functions within an environment of rapid and unrelenting change. The driving force behind this change is, of course, technology. Practically every day seems to bring new applications of electronics to the storage, organization, and communication of information. Online catalogs, fax, CD-ROM, electronic text scanning—they are now the stuff of our lives. They are altering, before our eyes, what we are doing and have been doing for years, decades, even centuries.

It is a heady and exciting time. New possibilities keep opening before us. Access to research library catalog records is no longer restricted by either time or place, only by the availability of a microcomputer and a telephone connection. Not only bibliographic files, but now full text in digitized form contained in the library collections, can be scanned and used by computer, either inside or outside the library. Copies of text can be sent electronically to any location with the necessary communication connections and equipment. Centuries-old limitations on access and availability are changing, practically overnight.

It is also a troubling time. As the changes pile one upon the next, we are not sure where they will end, nor what their ultimate consequences will be. We see them affecting, or potentially affecting, all aspects of scholarly communication: publication, distribution, use. We worry about dealing, according to our present practices, with more publication outside of normal channels, with less publication in print. We are concerned about being bypassed as scholars use their personal computers to query new electronic databases that have no need of libraries to store, organize, and maintain them.

We see a new world emerging, and we are not sure what it will be or how we will fit into it. What, we ask ourselves, will the research library be like ten, twenty, thirty years from now? What will research librarians be doing? We feel as though we are on a roller coaster over which we have little or no control, going at increasing speed to an uncertain destination. We are both exhilarated and anxious about the ride, and we're concerned about what awaits us at its end.

Will the research library survive? It is a question that seemed ridiculous a generation ago, but it no longer does. This book essentially began as I pondered that question, probed that threat of extinction. As I turned it over in my mind, it seemed to me that the threat extended beyond the research library to something else, something that was, in fact, the research library's reason for being: the accumulated and still accumulating record of scholarship.

After all, wasn't it this record, lodged in the world's research libraries, acquired and organized by research librarians, that was really in jeopardy? As more and more scholarly products were issued in electronic form and distributed through informal channels, what would happen to the integrity of the documentation of scholarship, which has been carefully preserved by research librarians for more than two millennia? Where would one turn to determine what had or had not been done on a particular question? Where would scholarship's consensual judgement, essential to its progress for centuries, be definitively maintained?

Clearly, although the concern was raised, quite properly, by technology, it was much more than a technological issue. It had to do with the function of the research librarian, the function of the scholar, and their relationships to scholarly information. Moreover, as I probed this issue further, it began to appear that, behind the evident opportunities that the new information technology offered and behind the ominous threats that seemed to lurk there, was a much greater opportunity, an opportunity to strengthen the record of scholarship and to improve the contribution that the research librarian makes to scholarship's advancement.

This opportunity was very much involved with the relationship of the research librarian to information, of the scholar to information, and of the librarian and the scholar to each other. These relationships were, I concluded, essential to the regular progress of scholarship. They had existed for centuries, since discovery began to be recorded and this record preserved, organized, and maintained. They had changed and developed over the years, in concert but also divided and almost at odds in interesting ways.

There was, it seemed, something of a contradiction in the approach of each to scholarly information. Furthermore, this contradiction seemed to be built into their different yet mutually essential responsibilities. As a consequence, there was a barrier between them, which was becoming increasingly evident as scholarship expanded and its record grew evermore complex. The new information technology seemed to offer the possibility of either a rise or a diminution in this barrier, depending upon how it was applied and used.

On the one hand, the new technology could undermine the integrity of the record of scholarship, making it more and more difficult for the librarian to gather it, to preserve it, and to organize it for use. On the other hand, technology could strengthen the record's integrity, making it easier to gather, preserve, and organize, and more readily available for use. How this choice could best be made required, it seemed, an understanding of how technology had influenced the librarian-scholar-information relationship in the past, and how it was influencing it at present.

It also became clear that a choice of this magnitude could not be made effectively by research librarians acting individually. In order to assess their ability to act in concert on such a matter, it was important to examine the tradition of cooperative or collaborative action on the part of research librarians, as well as the circumstances that appeared to make such action possible.

Finally, it became necessary to assess the possibilities that seemed to exist for research librarians to effect substantial change in an area that affected their most fundamental traditions, which was of considerable importance to, and which, in fact, required the assent and active involvement of, other major participants in the scholarly communication process.

This book is the result of this investigation and assessment. It is intended to be an analysis of the relationship between the research librarian, the scholar, and scholarly information. It utilizes knowledge about the past to assess the present and predict the future. It concludes with a broad-stroke description of the role and function of the research librarian and the nature of the research library in the electronic era.

The book ends, I believe, on an optimistic note. This may be, primarily, because I am an optimist. I am convinced, however, that there are adequate grounds for my optimism. I believe that research librarians have, within their power, the ability to meet the enormous challenges of the new technology, to capitalize upon its potential, and to strengthen their already-important contribution to the scholarly enterprise.

I must say a word or two about this book's bibliographic apparatus. Rather than follow the usual practice of incorporating citations in the text, I have prepared a bibliographic essay. I have done this for two reasons. First, regarding the text primarily as an argument, I wished to avoid the distraction that is endemic to the use of footnotes. Second, I wished to discuss the relevant literature to a degree that is difficult and cumbersome with in-text citations. An essay seemed to me to serve both of these purposes. The sequence of discussion in the bibliographic essay conforms to that of the main text.

1

The Librarian and Information

The orderliness of this process, the intellectual structure implicit in the library, the catalog, the index, the encyclopedia, the treatise, give meaning to the research in the past and motive for research in the future. The mere accumulation of miscellaneous details is not enough to provide such order and meaning.

J. M. Ziman

A research library . . . provides collections in depth. . . . Not only basic treatises, primary source materials, and the major journals are collected for its fields of instruction—as is the case in a college library—but the university library must also collect the secondary and tertiary sources, the background materials, the compendiums, the annotated and revised editions, the commentaries on commentaries, publications in remotely related fields, analyses from faulty as well as sound points of view—in short, a rather substantial portion of all the relevant thought on all subjects of interest to the university's young scholars and their mentors.

Rutherford D. Rogers
David C. Weber

Throughout their history, research librarians have functioned as the conservators of the record of scholarship. They have gathered and preserved the written, printed, and now electronically encoded information generated by the scholarly process as well as other information of immediate or potential value to research. In carrying out this role, research librarians have pursued two primary objectives: completeness and control. They have sought to gather collections that have included all—or as much as possible—of the scholarly record. They have also attempted to organize and structure these collections so that each component is adequately identified and appropriately positioned in relation to the whole.

For reasons quite beyond their control, research librarians have not fully achieved either of their objectives. They have not been able to preserve, in their individual libraries or collectively, the complete scholarly record; nor has it been possible for them to extend full and effective control over the record that they have preserved.

Furthermore, in carrying out their responsibilities, research librarians have been trapped by something of a paradox. Their responsibility for preservation and, subsequently, control has led them to restrict or make difficult the use of what they have so diligently preserved, the scholarly record.

It is and always has been the primary responsibility of the research librarian to acquire and maintain the record of scholarship. No one else in society can or does fulfill this function. Of course, millions of individuals and thousands of organizations possess portions of this record. The private collections of scholars and others, the inventories of new and antiquarian bookstores, the holdings of most public, academic, and other libraries—each of these contains a part of the scholarly record. It is, however, only the research librarian who has accepted as his or her responsibility the comprehensive gathering and preservation of recorded information that, taken together, documents the present state of scholarship.

In order to accomplish this, research librarians have sought to acquire as much as possible of total worldwide scholarly publication. This has not been a simple or easy task. Indeed, as scholarly production has continued to grow, acquisition of the scholarly record has become an intense, unabating, constantly expanding effort. Nevertheless, research librarians have persevered in its pursuit, and they have, by this process, developed extensive library collections, numbered in the millions of volumes. Together, these collections contain most of the scholarly record, an achievement of which research librarians can justifiably be very proud. This achievement is particularly noteworthy because it has been accomplished over a number of centuries by tens of thousands of librarians, located in many different and widely scattered libraries, who have functioned with little or no coordination beyond their common purpose.

Nevertheless, impressive as this achievement is, it has failed in its ultimate goal: conservation of the complete record of scholarship. In spite of all of their efforts, research librarians are aware that some portions of this record have been, and are continuing to be, lost.

As the scholarly record and research library collections have grown, an extensive bibliographic apparatus has been created to organize and control them. Research librarians have developed cataloging systems and classification schemes. The cataloging systems are intended to provide a descriptive inventory of the physically discrete items included in each library's collection, as well as author, title, and subject indexes to these holdings. The great classification schemes utilized in research libraries are classifications of knowledge. Designed to cover the entire spectrum of scholarly inquiry, research library classification schemes are an attempt to relate each item in each collection to its most relevant discipline and sub-discipline. These systems are supported with an array of bibliographies and indexes, developed by librarians and their colleagues in the information industry, whose objective is to cover comprehensively particular portions of recorded scholarship.

The ultimate purpose of this entire apparatus is to identify, as thoroughly and specifically as possible, every bit of recorded scholarly information available on any topic contained in the scholarly record. This identification is essential to use of the record. Without the control provided by the bibliographic apparatus, the scholarly record would be an unorganized mélange of miscellaneous scholarly products.

The bibliographic organization of research library collections has been the research librarian's second great achievement—as significant, in its way, as the gathering and maintenance of these collections. However, just as research librarians have not been able to acquire and preserve the complete record of scholarship, they have been unable to extend full and effective control over that record or even over the portion of that record that has been preserved. Because of this incompleteness, it is impossible to determine precisely how much of the record has been lost, although it is clear that the overwhelming portion has been retained.

Bibliographic systems are not the only means that librarians have developed to control and preserve their collections. Indeed, practically every aspect of research library activity is organized and structured to this end. Plans and profiles are established to guide collection development. Codes are devised for cataloging and classification. Policies govern access to and circulation of collections, as well as the reference services which are provided to assist clientele with their use.

Such systematization is designed to control not only the gathering and organization of collections, but their use as well. Indeed, throughout their history, research librarians have had to deal with a fundamental tension between preservation and use, between protecting and organizing the scholarly record and making it readily and easily available to its authors and primary users, the members of the scholarly community. This tension influences everything that the research librarian does.

Until quite recently, the interests of preservation generally prevailed over those of use. For centuries, research library policy and practice were designed specifically to limit use. Collections could be consulted only by selected individuals, usually selected by the librarian. Consultation was by appointment and was limited to the library. When regular use hours began to be provided, they were extremely brief. It is only within this century that research libraries have had extensive access hours.

Circulation of materials arrived more slowly than regular access hours. Throughout most of their history, research librarians resisted allowing items in their collections to be taken outside of the library. Major portions of research library collections still do not circulate; and many that do, circulate only for quite limited periods of time. Open stacks, which provide general access to the library's collections, were implemented in most research libraries later than circulation. Indeed, major portions of most research library collections remain closed or partially closed, including the central collections at some of these libraries.

The distribution of research library collections among branch libraries is also a relatively recent phenomenon, introduced generally within this century. This dissipation of control among an increasing number of physically-scattered units has been generally resisted by research librarians.

Far from reflecting idiosyncracies or predilections peculiar to librarians' personalities, as popular stereotypes have suggested, this emphasis on control is an inevitable consequence of the need to preserve the scholarly record. It provides the discipline that enables research librarians to manage the organization, maintenance, and use of research library collections with minimum threat to their preservation. Scholarly information is a chaos, out of which the research librarian is charged to bring order. Control is essential.

As controls over access to and use of research library collections have been relaxed, the complexity of these collections and of the apparatus designed to organize them has increased. Consequently, while research library collections have become easier to use in one respect, they have become much more difficult and demanding in another. Thus, the tension between preservation and use continues, albeit in a new and different form. Rather than being constrained primarily by policy, as in the past, research library use has come to be limited primarily by the library's complexity.

Effective use of the modern research library—use which goes beyond the need for a particular book or the answer to a specific and simple question—is quite demanding. A research library user who embarks upon an information search must, first of all, be familiar with the library's bibliographic apparatus. This means knowing not only the functions and organization of the library's catalogs, but also being aware of and knowledgeable about the myriad other catalogs, indexes, bibliographies, and related materials that comprise this apparatus. The user must understand the relationships among and between the various components of this apparatus.

To take a rather elementary example, users who are engaged in an information search involving the journal literature must understand that it is necessary to search for journal articles in journal indexes rather than in the library catalog. They must also know, however, that it is necessary to consult the library catalog in order to locate the particular journals containing the articles that their index search has identified.

If they are conducting a thorough and intensive subject search, it is important for research library users to be aware of the existence of specialized indexes and bibliographies relevant to the field. Those wishing to extend the search beyond the collections of the library they are using need to know about the availability of union catalogs as well as the catalogs of other particular libraries or collections.

In conducting an information search of any significant complexity, research library users have to be aware of a varied multiplicity of bibliographic sources that must be consulted. Furthermore, in working their way through this structure, users must be willing to move back and forth, identifying references in one source before determining their location and potential availability in another. They must, in effect, master the two-tiered organization of the research library's bibliographic apparatus, in which indexes and catalogs are linked only by the users' own perseverance and efforts.

The research library user must also understand library practices. This encompasses such varied matters as cataloging policy, circulation regulations, and interlibrary loan procedures. As no library represents its entire holdings in its main catalogs, it is important to understand what kinds of publications are most likely to be included, what supplementary catalogs or lists exist and what materials they cover, and what categories of material are entirely unrepresented.

To locate an item absent from its proper place on the shelves, the user must understand how to determine the reason for its absence and how, under those circumstances, to obtain the item or a copy of it. This may require a good deal of familiarity with library circulation policy and practice. Securing desired items may also require visits to several different locations, some of which may be at considerable distances from each other.

Information searches of this kind are arduous, complex, and time-consuming. To the uninitiated, they are frequently frustrating and seldom satisfying. Given the enormous wealth of materials available in a major research library, it is difficult to bring such a search to a close confident that all available relevant information sources have been exhausted. Moreover, the more knowledgeable a user is about the library and its holdings, the more likely he or she is to emerge from such a search literally overloaded with information. The user must then invest further time and effort winnowing out the portion or portions that are most relevant and useful to his or her particular need. Finally, because the record of scholarship and its bibliographic apparatus are both incomplete, no research library user, no matter how assiduous his or her efforts, can conclude a search confident that the entire state of scholarship on any question has been examined.

The complexity of the modern research library, although not designed for this purpose, has thus become a major impediment to its own use, at least to information searching that is more than highly specific or very casual. In an effort to address this, to bring the conflict between preservation and use into better balance, the research librarian offers assistance with use of the collection in the form of reference service.

Reference service did not originate, as a library function, in research libraries. Indeed, among all types of libraries, research libraries were the last to provide such service. Even when it was implemented, research library reference service was carefully and consciously restricted.

From its inception, reference service has been viewed by research librarians as assistance to users to better enable them to locate their own information. This self-service approach is a particularly interesting phenomenon in the history of research libraries. The question has frequently been posed, over the past several decades: why didn't the research librarian adopt an information-delivery mode similar to the special librarian, who has a tradition of packaging information to meet the clientele's particular needs?

A twofold response is generally offered. It is argued that the information needs of the scholarly community, who are the primary research library clientele, differ significantly from the needs of other library clienteles. Being expert in their fields, scholars do not and should not require extensive services from librarians, who lack such expertise. With respect to students, it is asserted that they, on their way to becoming scholars, need to learn how scholarly information is organized rather than have the information provided to them. As a consequence, the research library reference service offered to scholars has generally been limited to explanations of the bibliographic apparatus and how to use it. For students, this service has been extended to include library instruction in a variety of formats.

Although arguable, this position is not particularly convincing. The scholar certainly is expert in his or her field—far more expert than the research librarian. It is the librarian, however, who is expert in the library and its bibliographic apparatus; and it is the complexity of this apparatus that is at the root of the reference need. For the librarian to attempt to instruct the scholar in how to negotiate the bibliographic apparatus and the organization of the research library, every time the scholar seeks information, is rather like a physician instructing patients in medicine so that the latter can perform their own diagnosis and prescribe their own treatment. It is neither the most efficient nor the most effective way to provide medical treatment. Similarly, it is not efficient or effective for scholars to navigate the complexities of the bibliographic apparatus to secure their own information, advised and instructed by the librarian, when the librarian can do it much better.

With regard to students, it is quite correct that they are attending the research university in order to learn. Unless they are specifically interested in research librarianship, however, students are not there to learn about the intricacies of the research library and its bibliographic structure. It is small service for the librarian to assist students in negotiating these intricacies rather than provide them with the information that they need. The effort that students make in locating this information, assuming that they are successful, only intrudes upon and interferes with their primary learning activity.

Behind the arguments in favor of self-service are two other considerations, which are, perhaps, much more compelling determinants of research library information service policy. First, implementation of effective information service programs would require either a major increase in research library staffing or a major diversion of staff from other activities. Research librarians quite properly continue to place their emphasis on what has always been their primary responsibility: preserving the record of scholarship. Most of the research library's resources are directed to this goal. Staffing increases of the dimension necessary to provide information services have never been available to research libraries. Diversion of funds would reduce present programs to such an extent that preservation of the scholarly record would be fundamentally undermined. This would be an abdication by research librarians of their primary responsibility.

Second, extensive information service programs would increase, perhaps manyfold, the use of the scholarly record. This, in turn, would certainly increase the record's vulnerability, probably tipping the delicate preservation-use balance too far in the latter direction. Given these considerations, it can be argued that the research librarian's continued emphasis on the desirability of a self-service approach within the scholarly environment may, in fact, be a case of making a virtue of necessity. It is not that the research librarian could not benefit the scholarly community through the provision of such service; rather, it is that the consequent increased risk to preservation of the record of scholarship would be an unacceptable price to pay.

Thus, research librarians continue to struggle with preservation and use of the scholarly record, attempting to balance the requirements of one against the needs of the other. Throughout this struggle, they remain aware, as they must, that their primary consideration is, as it always has been, preservation. Yet they continue to seek means whereby use of the record can be made easier and more effective without jeopardizing its continued existence.

Research librarians also continue the struggle to achieve completeness and control. They know that both are presently beyond their grasp, even as they persevere in expanding collections as much as possible and in cataloging, classifying, and indexing these collections. They look to technology for ways to solve one or both of these problems, with the awareness that technological advance may actually increase and exacerbate them.

2

The Scholar and Information

Thus, the essential problems of scientific manpower and literature are twofold. At the top the critical problem is predominantly one of human engineering: arranging for the highest level people to interact in manageable numbers, seeing that the great journals continue to correspond to large natural groups, arranging for the important papers to be collected and compressed into standard monographs and texts. At the end it is one of switchboard operation: how does one manage the large body of scientists and appliers so that it keeps pace with the leaders; how does one monitor the lesser journals and the almost unnoticed papers so as to prevent wastage?

Derek J. De Solla Price

Later on, when the pressure slackened a bit, I attempted to adopt the normal routine of checking through learned journals. I soon cut down on that activity, not because I regarded the articles as useless, but for the opposite reason: I was interested in everything, everything seemed to have some relevance to my interests, and yet the pursuit of knowledge in all directions at once was impracticable.... Nevertheless, I went through a long period in which every publication of mine was followed by neurotic fears of being confronted with proof of having plagiarized it from some source I had not read.

Northrup Frye

Scholars are the producers and primary consumers of scholarly information. Their writings, which report the results of their experiments and investigations, become part of the record of scholarship. In conducting these experiments and carrying out these investigations, the scholars draw upon the reports of others, contained in that record. In their use of the record, they are primarily interested in two things: convenience and reliability. They want to secure the information they need as easily as possible. They must also rely on the accuracy and sufficiency of this information.

Although they constantly seek to achieve both convenience and reliability, convenience has a particularly high value to scholars. It is for this reason that, whenever possible, they avoid using the research library and its bibliographic apparatus. Scholars value the library as the repository of the record of scholarship, but they are unwilling to invest the time and effort necessary to conduct most of their information searching there. Rather, they have developed, and usually pursue alternate, more convenient means.

Unfortunately, these means do not yield the reliability that the scholar also seeks. Although this risk is present for all members of the scholarly community, it is particularly prevalent for students, beginning scholars, and, most of all, inactive scholars. Unable to reconcile convenience and reliability, the scholar continues to pursue the former and risk the latter. As a consequence, a measure of uncertainty continues to qualify the relationship between the scholar and scholarly information.

The primary aim of scholars is to produce new information that will be recognized by their colleagues and accepted as knowledge. To accomplish this, scholars must write reports of their findings and submit these reports for review and publication. These reports then become part of the record of scholarship, where they are referred to and utilized by others who pursue related investigations or simply seek to keep pace with their fields. By this process, the scholar is both the producer and the primary consumer of scholarly information.

As consumers, scholars are particularly interested in any and all information that has a bearing upon their own work. They must remain current with the state of scholarship in their specialty and in related fields. If he or she is actively engaged in research, the scholar is particularly concerned with investigations by others that may be particularly relevant to his or her own. For beginning scholars, this concern is, necessarily, broader and more active. For those who are inactive but, because of teaching or other responsibilities, maintain an interest in their field, this concern may be less intense and less intensively pursued—but it is pursued nonetheless.

In their search for information, scholars are interested in two things, reliability and convenience. Reliability is, of course, a fundamental requirement of scholarship. If the information on which it is based cannot be trusted, the findings and, consequently, the value of the scholarly contribution are suspect. To be reliable, the information must be accurate and the search must be thorough. Inaccurate or omitted relevant information jeopardizes the quality and acceptance of the work.

Convenience is also important for the scholar. The active scholar is usually a very busy person. In most instances, he or she has teaching or other responsibilities in addition to research. Because scholarship is, to a considerable extent, competitive, the scholar is concerned about concluding his or her research expeditiously. Recognition, advancement, income, security—all can hinge to a considerable extent on the ability of the scholar to be the first in the field to announce a particular discovery. If another scholar makes an announcement first, he or she will lose not only the benefits that would result from the discovery, but also the time invested in pursuing the research.

Consequently, scholars want to spend as little time as possible consulting the scholarly record. They want precisely the information they need and no more. They do not want to extract this information by combing all possible or even all available sources. This does not mean that they want knowingly to ignore anything that is relevant to their investigation. Quite the contrary. However, they are not willing to pursue extensive quests through the literature in order to discover everything that may have any bearing on their work. In particular, scholars avoid using the research library, where the record of scholarship has been gathered, maintained, and organized with great effort and care over many, many years.

There has been considerable investigation, by librarians and others, concerning use of the library and its bibliographic apparatus by scholars in all disciplines. The findings of these studies, which have been carried out principally in Great Britain and the United States, have been remarkably consistent. They have also demonstrated the accuracy of many librarians' perceptions: that scholars utilize library collections remarkably little, the bibliographic apparatus even less, and librarians' reference services hardly at all.

Studies of research library collection use indicate that considerably less than one-half of their contents are consulted by scholars or others within any twelve-month period. Indeed, the active portion of humanities collections has been identified as 40 percent or less, and the active portion of social science collections has been estimated at 25 percent. For the sciences, it has been suggested that 10 percent of research library collections account for 80 percent of use. Other studies have concluded that one-third to one-half of research library collections may never be consulted during their entire existence in the library.

Citation analysis, which would seem to be an even more reliable basis for judgments about scholarly research practices, has found that the vast majority of references identified in all fields and disciplines relates to only a small portion of scholarly journal publication—the "core" journals that are generally subscribed to directly by scholars. In science, 90 percent of references have been found to be clustered in 10 percent of the journals. In the social sciences, 12 percent of the journals account for 75 percent of the citations, and 75 percent of the references in humanities are derived from 20 percent of the journals.

Perhaps even more enlightening are surveys of scholars' research methods. One extensive study, covering all major disciplinary areas, concluded that scholars drew upon their own collections for 58 percent of their cited sources, as opposed to deriving 21 percent from library collections. A relatively recent national survey found that 71 percent of the humanities and social science scholars queried had utilized only their personal collections to conduct their most recent research. Such investigations clearly indicate that scholars in all disciplines resist using libraries, preferring to rely on their own collections and their personal or departmental journal subscriptions as much as possible.

Analyses have also concluded that scholars make even less use of library catalogs, indexes, abstracts, and bibliographies than they do of library collections. These analyses have been numerous. Some have covered all scholarly disciplines; others have focused, respectively, on the sciences, social sciences, and humanities, while still others have examined patterns in particular fields and specialties. The inescapable conclusion from these studies is that the bibliographic apparatus, which has absorbed, and continues to absorb, much time and effort on the part of research librarians, is not simply ignored but actively avoided by scholars.

Least used of all library services offered to scholars is reference service. This has been documented in a number of studies, many of them quite extensive, covering all disciplines. As with the investigations of scholars' use of the research library bibliographic apparatus, these findings suggest active rather than passive avoidance.

Various conclusions have been drawn from the respective findings. It has been suggested that the research library's capabilities and services are not adequately advertised, that they are uneven in quality, and even that they are ineffective. If these findings are viewed together, however, a very different judgment seems far more justified: the processes of library research are far too distracting and time-consuming to be generally acceptable to scholars.

Scholars do not avoid turning to the research librarian because they believe that the librarian will not be helpful. Quite the contrary, they are concerned that the librarian will provide too much help. While scholars seek to find the particular pieces of information that they need as quickly as possible, with a minimum of effort or diversion, the librarian is most likely to identify the maximum number of available sources and strategies, substantially expanding the potential scope of the search. As the scholar will still have to do the actual searching and as the librarian's self-service philosophy makes him or her reluctant to suggest one source or strategy over another, the scholar finds little benefit in seeking the librarian's assistance.

Furthermore, scholars are not confident in their ability to judge the effectiveness of a search using the library's bibliographic apparatus. After all, this apparatus is not a scholar's creation; it is the work of librarians and their colleagues in information organization, bibliographers and indexers. Not understanding the mysteries of its intricate structure, the scholar is as uncertain in using or evaluating the librarian's apparatus as the librarian would be if he or she were expected to make judgments about the quality or importance of the scholar's research.

This is not to suggest that scholars do not value research libraries or the effort that research librarians have invested, and continue to invest, in gathering, organizing, and maintaining the scholarly record. This record is of central importance to the scholarly community. Publication documents the results of research. Publication by a refereed journal or press authenticates the contribution. Citations in each work relate it to other works. The scholarly record is, at once, a means of maintaining currency, a source for particular information, and the ultimate authority on the state of scholarship as well as the contributions of individual scholars.

Nevertheless, the research library is the last, rather than the first, place to which scholars generally turn when seeking information. And when he or she does use the library, the scholar uses it in ways that tend to baffle and confuse librarians. Scholars largely ignore the bibliographic apparatus that the librarian has painstakingly created and assembled. Rather, they proceed, in apparently helter-skelter fashion, to locate information by other means. They browse recent journals. They browse the stacks. They visit special collections. They utilize the catalog, if at all, primarily to locate particular, pre-identified items. They generally invest little time in the entire process. The highly structured formality that the research librarian has been at great pains to develop, and which is essential to the organization and maintenance of the record of scholarship, functions not as a help but a barrier, dividing the scholar from the research library and librarian.

Furthermore, even the kinds of interest that scholars typically show in the library do not demonstrate a predilection to capitalize upon its extensive collections or complex organization. Although some scholars seem to place high value on carrels in the library, these are often infrequently used. Furthermore, when they are used, it is more as a hideaway, in which to read and write, than because of their proximity to library materials. On the whole, scholars stay away from libraries, preferring, when necessary, to send research assistants in their place. Indeed, for most scholars, interaction with the library tends to focus on what are, perhaps, best described as administrative or operational matters: designating materials to be put on reserve, requesting that a particular title be added to the collection, urging that a particular title be cataloged promptly.

Of course, every research librarian is familiar with scholars who are frequently in the library. They usually pay particular attention to the collections, often to a special collection. They sometimes take an almost personal interest in the library's ambiance and efficiency. They become well known to members of the library staff. Such scholars tend to serve on library committees or represent their departments to the library. They are seen—by librarians, by their colleagues, and by academic administrators—as spokespersons on library matters. These library-oriented scholars play an important political role; however, when they actually use the library, their patterns of use generally differ little from those of their more distant colleagues.

Perhaps most indicative of scholars' views of the library is the issue that seems to rank first among their library concerns: their inability to locate a particular item that they need. Whether it is not in the library's collections, or charged out to someone else, or lost—whatever the reason—the unavailability of a book at time of need is generally recognized by scholars to be the research library's most serious shortcoming.

This is because, in the final analysis, the scholar does expect the research library to be what it continually, and unsuccessfully, strives to be: the repository of the complete record of scholarship. Scholars can accept many other defects—the library's complexity, its rules and regulations, even its emphasis on self-service—but they cannot accept its incompleteness. The research library is, after all, the scholar's final resort. It is where he or she goes after other sources of information have been found wanting. Scholars want to rely on the library, and are particularly disappointed whenever they find that they cannot.

Rather than using the library as a primary source for information regarding the status of scholarship on any particular issue, scholars have developed their own alternative information-seeking methods. First, they gather information from other scholars. As students, they depend upon professors. Beginning scholars turn to more advanced scholars, through maintaining connections at the institutions where they did their graduate work, through newly established relationships with colleagues at the institutions with which they have become affiliated, or through conferences and symposia. As scholars contribute and continue to contribute to the knowledge of their fields, they achieve recognition and establish network connections with peers at other institutions. Those scholars who achieve the greatest distinction often become the leaders in their networks.

Second, scholars follow citation trails through the literature. This is an extremely important method for students, who pursue it most aggressively in connection with their dissertations. It is also important for beginning scholars, before they become actively involved in networks. Even for the most advanced and respected scholars, citation-directed searching is never abandoned as an information-seeking mechanism; although scholars of this eminence tend to rely on junior colleagues or research assistants to do most of the actual work.

Finally, scholars maintain currency with their specialties and their disciplines as a whole by regularly browsing the important journals in their fields. Usually, these are journals to which they subscribe, although they may share journals within their departments or even rely, to some extent, on library subscriptions. Students and beginning scholars, particularly, depend upon library or departmental subscriptions, as do many inactive scholars. When scholars achieve eminence, they are often invited to join editorial boards, where they gather more advanced knowledge about, as well as influence over, new information that is submitted for publication.

Scholars' methods are not without their problems and deficiencies. Their information-access system is, first of all, an unequal system. It heavily favors some members of the scholarly community over others. It performs most effectively for advanced and established scholars, who are estimated to comprise only a very small portion, perhaps 5 percent, of the scholarly community. This scholarly elite is relatively well served by processes which, coupled with their own continuing scholarly activity, keep them apprised of developments in their fields.

For students or beginning scholars, there are much more visible information-access problems. Early in their careers, scholars are far more uncertain, about their own knowledge and about the knowledge of those to whom they can turn, than they will be when they are more recognized and established. Consequently, students or beginning scholars are forced to rely much more heavily on browsing and citation searching than they will later in their careers.

Those members of the scholarly community who are least well served by scholarship's information-access systems are the inactive scholars. Without the mentor relationships enjoyed by students and beginning scholars, and generally denied access to networks, inactive scholars must rely almost entirely on browsing and citation searching in the literature—a reliance which becomes steadily less certain as protracted inactivity weakens the scholar's quality of judgement about the current state of research in the field. Yet even the most advanced and distinguished scholars have expressed concerns about the possibility that they have, perhaps, overlooked useful information that more extended searching might have uncovered. There are few, but nonetheless important, examples in the history of scholarship of relevant information that have been overlooked by such scholars, leading sometimes to significant problems with or delays in the advancement of knowledge. There are also enough continuing examples of redundant findings—most of which result in loss of time, effort, and perhaps recognition; a few of which lead to scandal—to make even the most self-confident scholar occasionally nervous.

It is also the case that the scholar's regular information-seeking methods do not provide an answer to every question. This may result in a weakening of the value of the research. Indeed, it may even contribute to the abandonment of an otherwise productive line of inquiry. In at least some of these instances, it may well be that a more comprehensive approach to information searching would have contributed to a better result.

Scholars generally recognize that their information-seeking systems are imperfect; however, they have been unable to identify a viable remedy. Convenience has become so important that most scholars are willing to accept a certain amount of risk, relying on their knowledge of their field, including who is working on what topic, rather than invest the enormous amount of time and effort required for comprehensive searching, particularly if this means depending upon an apparatus that they do not truly understand.

Nor does technology seem to offer a viable solution. Recent experiments with electronic data storage and transmission have proved, at best, to be a mixed bag of generally marginal benefits together with significantly increased problems. The improvements in convenience have been more than offset by increases in information overload. Some of these experiments have indicated the need for a filter to screen and package incoming information.

In the meantime, the volume and complexity of scholarly information continues to grow exponentially, making it increasingly difficult for even the most active scholars to keep up. Moreover, more and more of this information is dispensed in formats that bypass standard publication routes, such as reports, manuscripts, preprints, and, most recently, electronic mail. Not only does such distribution elude the peer-review authentication that is a critical element of the standard scholarly publication process; it also creates a body of material with limited distribution which is poorly indexed and difficult to locate or even identify.

The scholarly community has attempted to deal with this expansion of activity in a number of ways. There is a continuing subdivision of disciplines into an increasing number of specialties, some of which incorporate cross-disciplinary connections. Many of these specialties have established journals, which are intended to keep their subscribers informed of the significant scholarly contributions in those specialties and free them from the need to monitor a number of different publications. Other journals have appeared whose primary purpose is to provide information about research in process. Scholars travel increasingly, exchanging information through seminars and conferences.

Despite all of these efforts, effective information access continues to be a problem. The basic weakness remains: scholars have only a limited amount of time to absorb information, even very useful information, if they are to proceed with their research. The conflict between convenience and reliability remains unresolved, and it continues to be an important feature of the relationship between the scholar, scholarly information, and the custodian of that information, the research librarian.

3

The Influence of Technology

Primary objectification occurred at the stage of written information, the secondary objectification took place at the stage of printed information, and the tertiary objectification was initiated with the electronic processing of information.

Yoneji Masuda

It is seen to be quite proper to call the use of an inanimate invention a cause of social change, though it could not be a cause without the active manipulation of it by a human being.

William F. Ogburn

The nature of the record of scholarship, together with the primary characteristics of its maintenance and use, have been, throughout history, largely determined by the state of information technology. Indeed, technology has established both the possibilities and the limits for recording, exchanging, and securing access to scholarly information. Information technology is now entering its third epoch. Each of these eras—manuscript, print, and now electronic—has provided opportunities to extend the capabilities of the scholarly record, and each has posed new problems as well.

Invention of the manuscript made possible the creation of a lasting, usable record of scholarship. It also severely limited its accessibility and reliability, primarily because portions of this record were widely scattered, protectively guarded, and often inconsistent. Printing substantially improved physical accessibility and reliability; however, the entire record remained dispersed and its organization became increasingly complex. Electronic storage and transmission of information provide the capability to enhance accessibility further, but also to undermine the order and coherence achieved during the print era.

Information technology has also largely determined the role and function of the research librarian. Throughout the manuscript era, the librarian was primarily a conservator, whose attention was concentrated on gathering and preserving the record of scholarship. During the print era, the research librarian's role expanded to include organization of that record. Now, in the early stages of the electronic era, the research librarian is being challenged to find new means to preserve the scholarly record in the face of potential information anarchy.

Technological invention first made it possible for information to be recorded and, therefore, distributed and retained. Subsequently, technology has improved and enlarged this capability through three major advances. Each of these developments has expanded the possibilities for distribution and use of the scholarly record, and each has posed new challenges as to how that record can be organized and accessed.

The three technological developments which have exerted major influence on the record of scholarship are, respectively: the written manuscript, the printed book, and the electronic tape or disk. Each dominates and largely defines an important era in scholarly communication.

The manuscript era was the first period in which scholarship could be conveniently recorded, preserved, and disseminated. The findings of scholarship were set down on vellum or paper. In this form, they were made available to other scholars and to students. Copies were made, allowing for further distribution. These copies were retained, usually in collections that included other scholarly works.

Manuscripts were disseminated through a variety of means. Itinerant scholars and students carried copies with them on their travels, sometimes trading them for other manuscripts, sometimes making them available for copying, often in exchange for permission to make copies of other manuscripts themselves. As demand increased, professional copyists appeared, augmenting the number of copies available and further increasing their dissemination. Manuscripts became a desirable commodity, the object of barter and trade.

In these ways, the record of scholarship was begun. However, there were severe limits to the accessibility of this record. In order to be retained, disseminated, or used, scholarly information had to be packaged in the form of a manuscript. As a result, the information also became, as it were, imprisoned in its vehicle. A scholar seeking information had to determine that it was contained in a particular manuscript, discover where that manuscript was kept, and then travel to consult it.

None of this was easy. Records of manuscript holdings were limited, sketchy, unreliable, and difficult to obtain. Scholars usually had to rely on information that they secured from other scholars, which, itself, often involved considerable effort. Nor could such information always be trusted. Travel was arduous and time-consuming. Even after these hurdles had been overcome, and the scholar had arrived where the manuscript was held, it was not always certain that permission to see it would be granted.

Copying required special permission, which was frequently not given. Indeed, it was usually essential for anyone seeking to consult or copy a manuscript to be known to its owner, either personally or by reputation, or to have an important or influential sponsor. Even well-known or well-authenticated scholars were denied access to desired materials, sometimes at the same time that other items were made available to them. Such decisions could be quite arbitrary.

Due to the nature of manuscript copying, there was usually some—and frequently a great deal of—variation among copies of the same work. Such variety increased as more and more copyists were employed. Because they seldom had opportunity for comparisons between the copy and the original, scholars were usually unaware of the nature or degree of variation in any of the manuscripts they used.

The descriptions of manuscript items that existed were typically brief, frequently unreliable, and shared no common, understood standards as to form or content. There was, of course, no comprehensive listing of the entire record of scholarship.

The invention of printing substantially expanded the possibilities for distribution of the scholarly record. Publication was quicker, easier, and much more economical than had been the case during the manuscript period. Many more titles were produced, each in editions of multiple copies. Most of these copies were exact replications of each other. Books began to be distributed widely, at costs far below those of manuscripts, and collections grew. These collections soon contained many times the titles present in even the largest manuscript collections.

As scholarship expanded, procedures were created by the scholarly community to review and authenticate contributions in advance of publication. Scholarly societies and universities became the primary scholarly publishers. Functioning through editors and reviewers, these publishers established and implemented standards for admitting contributions to the recognized body of knowledge.

Despite the enormous improvements of the print era, some of the limitations on the scholarly record that were endemic to manuscripts persisted into and through the later period. Most important, scholarship was still produced and distributed in packages. Although the printed book was a much superior package in almost every respect, it nevertheless shared the manuscript's primary limitation: it had to be physically possessed in order to be used.

In addition, a new and increasingly troubling problem appeared during the print era. As the record of scholarship expanded, it became more and more demanding to organize, control, and use. Complexity became a critical problem for the users of the scholarly record as the print period progressed.

The electronic era is ushering in a new means of access to the scholarly record. In electronic form, scholarly information does not have to be distributed in manuscript or print packages. A single copy of an electronic record can be made available, easily and practically instantaneously, to any user, wherever he or she is located. This access can be as selective or as comprehensive as desired. It can involve the transfer of portions of the record in electronic form or the generation of hard copy at the point of receipt.

Consequently, it is not necessary to distribute copies of an electronic record in order to ensure convenient access. On the contrary, a single record can perform the same access function that required many redundant print or manuscript copies. Indeed, it can perform this function better, because the user does not have to come to wherever the copy is held in order to get needed information; such information can be secured electronically from wherever the user is located.

However, this new freedom of access is also bringing its own problems. Because electronic communication of text is becoming so easy, it is no longer necessary to use traditional channels for the distribution of scholarly information. Every scholar can, in effect, broadcast findings as he or she wishes. This threatens to overwhelm the procedures established over several centuries to control and validate scholarly communication.

Indeed, the traditional functions of publisher, reviewer, and editor are potentially in jeopardy. It does not seem likely that the system carefully built up during the print period, for review and authentication of scholarly products, can continue to manage dispersal of scholarly information in an electronic environment. These changes are, of course, bringing an array of new challenges and opportunities for the entire scholarly community, including the research librarian.

Just as the nature and capabilities of the record of scholarship have changed over time, due to the impact of technological developments, so the functions and responsibilities of the research librarian have been modified and transformed by what has happened to the scholarly record. And just as the progressive alterations in the scholarly record can be observed as enlargements of its capability, so the research librarian's role has developed and expanded proportionately.

During the manuscript era, the research librarian's primary responsibilities were gathering and preserving scholarly records. The librarian acquired manuscripts by gift and purchase, but mostly by trade and copying. Visiting scholars would bring manuscripts to trade, or they would bring manuscripts to copy while they copied in exchange. The librarian was usually a scholar, and might also travel, bringing personal copies for similar exchanges.

Once acquired, manuscripts were carefully protected and preserved. Indeed, preservation was so important during the manuscript era that it might well be described as the preservation period in the history of research librarianship. Access was extremely limited and closely supervised, and it was invariably within the confines of the library. Much of the time invested by research librarians in their libraries was devoted to screening would-be users and monitoring use. The librarian also supervised copyists, and may even have invested a portion, sometimes a considerable portion, of his or her time in copying.

Bibliographic control was primitive, largely because the relatively modest collections of the manuscript era required nothing more. The major bibliographic records were generally sketchy lists which some libraries maintained as inventories. Although such lists might occasionally be copied or exchanged, scholars most often became aware of the existence and location of particular works or their copies through communication with other scholars.

Acquisition and preservation continued as major responsibilities for the research librarian well into and, indeed, throughout the print era. As publication expanded, acquisition became more complex and time-consuming. Toward the end of the era, research libraries all had sizable staffs of librarians and others to identify, select, and acquire materials for their collections. Such acquisition was primarily by purchase, but gift and exchange were also important. Copying, now in the form of reprints and photocopies, reasserted itself late in the print era.

Each print library contained a substantial representation of the total scholarly record, many times larger than even the most extensive manuscript library. A significant and steadily-increasing portion of these collections, including the most used and respected scholarly publications, was replicated in more and more libraries. These developments vastly improved the availability and reliability of the record of scholarship.

As a consequence, the necessary redundancy of collections among manuscript libraries continued—indeed, on a far grander scale than before—throughout the print period. Similarly, although the distribution system for books was a great improvement over manuscript distribution, neither system could ensure that every portion of the scholarly record was readily available or even that it would be preserved.

Access to research library collections became progressively easier and more convenient. Restrictions on use, although they continued to be rather severe through most of the print era, were more relaxed and regularized than they had been during the manuscript period. More library collections were established. These collections were much nearer at hand and easier to reach than manuscript collections had been. Preservation became more challenging during the print era, as circulation was provided, stack access extended, and collections distributed among multiple locations. Large staffs were required to maintain and control these collections. Preservation came to include a number of activities, such as circulation, stack maintenance, and reserve. All of these functions shared the common goal of overseeing the collection and monitoring its use.

It was organization of the collection, however, that became the dominant and characteristic function in this, the second period in the development of research librarianship. In fact, all significant bibliographic control activities were devised or invented during this era, and they were continuously expanded and refined until its close.

As scholarly publication increased and research library collections grew, the scholarly record became more and more complicated, and so did research library collections. Proper maintenance of and access to these collections required more than the relatively simple inventories maintained in manuscript libraries. These were replaced by detailed descriptive cataloging, extensive subject cataloging, systematic classification, and indexing. Catalogs of major collections were printed and disseminated, initially in book form but subsequently in card form as well. This apparatus gradually became as complex as the collections it was designed to organize, and as difficult to use. With continued growth, these systems and schemes became more and more complex. Increasingly large and specialized staffs were employed to carry out these functions.

It is difficult to overemphasize the importance of bibliographic control to research librarians, to their libraries, and, indeed, to continued maintenance of the scholarly record, during the print period. Without the bibliographic apparatus, it would be literally impossible for research librarians to manage the scholarly record, and neither research libraries nor a usable record would exist.

The enlarged size and complexity of the scholarly record and its bibliographic apparatus during the print era made it necessary for research librarians to assist scholars and students in their use of the library collections. Reference programs were implemented. The number of research librarians involved in this activity increased, but never became large, particularly in comparison with the number of librarians and support staff who were engaged in preservation and bibliographic control. And, even with the expansion of this activity to include library instruction, reference did not come to assume a major role among research librarian functions during the print era.

During the electronic era, research librarians will confront substantial new challenges in carrying out their responsibilities. The ease of distribution of recorded information during this period, which is increasingly bypassing established processes, will make preservation of the scholarly record increasingly difficult. It will not be possible to rely on the print era's publication-distribution channels to gather individual records in order to assemble them into collections. As more and more "publications" are circulated through informal and irregular channels, it will become harder and harder for librarians to identify them, track them down, and acquire them. Consequently, as the electronic era moves forward, the research librarian will have to seek a new and different approach in order to respond to its new requirements.

The nucleus of such an approach is, however, present in the capabilities of electronic information transfer. Just as the new technology makes it easy to distribute scholarly products outside of established channels, it also provides for widespread access to a single electronic record, in lieu of its distribution through multiple print copies. This, in turn, makes a new and improved mode of gathering and maintaining the scholarly record potentially viable.

Instead of gathering hundreds of partially incomplete and largely redundant collections in individual research libraries, it will be possible to assemble a single, comprehensive electronic record at one location, from where it can be made generally accessible. Certainly, establishing a consolidated electronic record will be a monumental task to plan, negotiate, and implement. On the other hand, it may be the only available way of continuing to preserve the scholarly record, as the electronic era progresses and more and more of this record is produced in electronic form.

With a consolidated electronic record, requirements for maintenance of the bibliographic apparatus will change as well. Rather than the complex, two-tiered, multiform, overlapping, and incomplete structure required by the print era, the electronic apparatus can be single, unified, and complete. Its content index can be directly linked to catalog information describing each and every work contained in the record, whether it is a monograph, a journal article, a report, or something else. Identification of physical volumes will no longer be necessary, because, with an electronic record, physical volumes will be meaningless. The index can be as detailed and extensive as the index of a book. Indeed, an electronic bibliographic apparatus for an electronic scholarly record would, in effect, become a single enormous index to a single enormous database. Such an accomplishment would, obviously, carry research librarians a major step forward in their quest to achieve completeness of and control over the record of scholarship.

As they move forward into the electronic era, research librarians face an extremely consequential choice, certainly the most consequential in their history. They can continue to function as they have in a print environment, seeking to gather and preserve copies of scholarly products as more and more of these products become electronic. They can struggle to adapt increasingly outmoded practices to new conditions, as the scholarly record which they have played such a critical role in achieving and maintaining gradually loses its integrity. Conversely, they can take advantage of the new technology in order to maintain and even improve the record's integrity. Accomplishing this will be a formidable task. It will require, more than anything else, an intense, committed, collaborative effort on the part of all research librarians. Its alternative, however, may well be dissolution of the record of scholarship as well as the research library.

4

From Cooperation to Collaboration

The question is relevant to any future information strategies we may devise: to what degree are we willing to modify or even dismantle comfortable ways of thinking and acting in order to accommodate the new technology?

Wilson P. Dizard

The essence of leadership is choice, a singularly individual act in which a person assumes responsibility for a commitment to direct an organization along a particular path.

Abraham Zaleznik

Although conservation of the record of scholarship is a responsibility that has been common to all research librarians, it has not been approached in a collaborative manner. Rather, it has been practiced separately, redundantly, and even competitively in individual research libraries. As a consequence, the complete scholarly record has not been preserved, while major portions of it have been widely replicated. Other portions of the record are scattered, tucked away in individual collections, often with little or no generally-available bibliographic coverage.

Research librarians have not made substantial efforts to change this situation. Rather, the history of research libraries has been a history of individual development, with little organized or sustained cooperation. Serious and effective research library cooperation is scarcely one hundred years old, and the most substantial programs have been implemented during the latter part of this century. Furthermore, even these activities have occurred within the context of continued independent development, reinforcing rather than weakening the primary emphasis on local priorities.

No incident better illustrates the problems endemic to research library cooperation in a print-dominated information environment than the failure of the proposed National Periodicals Center. At the same time, examination of the reasons for this failure clearly offers valuable instruction to research librarians as they explore the viability of a new, collaborative approach to management of the scholarly record in the developing electronic environment.

From the very beginning, research librarians throughout the world have shared responsibility for preserving and maintaining the record of scholarship. No single library possesses, or has even come close to possessing, the entire record. As a consequence, no research library can provide assurance to its users that the precise information they need will be available to them from its collections, even if the user conducts an extensive search.

Furthermore, every research library possesses some materials that are represented in no other library, as well as other items that are available from only a limited number of other libraries. Many of these works are not recorded in union catalogs and other forms of shared library holdings information. Even determining the existence of such items, let alone locating and securing access to them, is often difficult and time-consuming, with a result that is by no means certain.

Providing access to each other's collections is a relatively late development in the history of research libraries, and its practice has been generally discouraged. Regular interlibrary loan activity among research libraries is scarcely one hundred years old. During most of this time, and even today in many research libraries, interlibrary lending units have been poorly staffed, not usually advertised to clientele, and their service points have been tucked away in odd corners of large and complex library facilities.

Clientele have frequently, themselves, been expected to gather whatever information might be available regarding the particular libraries that might possess the materials they need. Once this information has been obtained, research librarians have followed complex and time-consuming protocols in order to secure these items. Most libraries have placed restrictions upon the types of material that can be borrowed from them, as well as upon the terms and conditions of its use. Research libraries often charge each other for providing access to their collections via interlibrary loan.

Research librarians have not been significantly more hospitable to scholars affiliated with other institutions who have appeared on their doorstep, seeking access to their collections. Unless the visiting scholar has some form of entrée, such as sponsorship by a local faculty member or a request for privileges from the library director at his or her home institution, he or she is likely to secure only limited access. At many research libraries, all visitors will be charged a fee, often a substantial one, no matter who vouched for them.

There are very good reasons for research librarians to restrict and discourage access to their collections, particularly on the part of other libraries' clientele. Loss of or damage to parts of its holdings potentially reduces a research library's ability to provide for its own clientele and certainly diminishes its coverage of the scholarly record. Such loss or damage is a constant serious threat, and it is only enlarged if access is extended beyond those to whom the library owes an explicit obligation.

Because drawing upon the resources of other libraries has been such a difficult matter for librarians and scholars alike, research librarians have concentrated on building their local collections to the maximum extent possible. This has produced a high level of duplication among these collections.

Every research library acquires the core scholarly publications in almost every field. This material tends to be particularly expensive, including, as it does, a large number of journals, indexes, and reference materials. As a consequence, a substantial amount of research libraries' acquisition funds are regularly invested in widely replicated holdings, leaving more peripheral items to the much more uncertain fate of selection processes driven by local interests and constrained by scarce resources. Under these circumstances, it is not surprising that this portion of the scholarly record is widely distributed among research libraries, with no assurance that a particular item is available anywhere. Some of this material, deemed of peripheral value even by its owners, may be unrepresented or poorly represented in that library's own bibliographic apparatus.

The emphasis placed by research librarians on local considerations has led to a competitive approach to research library development. This competitiveness is particularly evident in the close attention that research librarians give to the annual publication of comparative research library data. Nor is this competitive instinct limited to librarians. Research university faculty and administrators also monitor research library data, as evidenced by the regular, and sometimes inaccurate, summaries of that data in higher education media.

Indeed, it has been vigorously and effectively argued that collection size data is one of the best indicators of the relative stature among research universities. Most university library administrators are personally acquainted with the interest that faculty and university administrators display in such data, just as they are not, themselves, averse to utilizing it to justify increased library support.

It is clear that this competitive approach to research library development has been an important factor in furthering individual research library growth, particularly in times of scholarly expansion, such as the decades following the end of World War II. It is not equally evident, however, that such competition has contributed to the success of the research librarian's ultimate task, preservation of the record of scholarship. Certainly, it has intensified the librarian's natural primary focus on local objectives, and it has further diminished whatever inclination he or she may otherwise have had to seek a more collaborative means of preserving the scholarly record.

Research library cooperation has neither a long nor a particularly proud history. Zealous advocates of cooperation may discern early inclinations in medieval manuscript copying or in some limited exchanges of resources during the early centuries of the print era; however, closer examination reveals more evidence of selfish barter than of altruistic common effort in these activities. Indeed, it seems to be generally recognized that serious interest in cooperation among research libraries did not begin until approximately a century ago.

This was, of course, a time of accelerating research library growth. Spurred by rapid expansions in research and higher education, scholarly publication flourished. Research library collections multiplied. Indeed, they had already reached sufficient size to require the development of detailed, comprehensive classification schemes and rigorously standardized cataloging codes. Research librarians began to be concerned about their ability to acquire and maintain the scholarly record.

Important cooperative activities were undertaken by research libraries at this time, including organized interlibrary lending and the beginnings of shared cataloging, through the exchange of catalog cards. Much more far-reaching possibilities were discussed. Among these, the most revolutionary was certainly the establishment of a national library of record—a library which would be responsible for acquiring and maintaining the entire record of scholarship, thus allowing each research library to focus entirely and selectively upon local needs.

This proposal was discussed with some vigor in a variety of forums as the nineteenth century wound to a close. In fact, two different models were considered: a single, comprehensive library, or several regional libraries. Neither model was implemented, although the Library of Congress came to assume some features of the single-library proposal. It might also be argued that the regional-library concept was at least partially implemented *de facto* with the growth of the very largest academic research libraries; however, the geographic distribution of these libraries together with their continued predominant local focus makes such an argument difficult to sustain.

Throughout the present century, research library cooperation has proceeded, usually slowly and often haltingly. There have been a number of successes, including shared cataloging (Library of Congress printed cards followed by the MARC database, the Online Computer Library Center, and the Research Libraries Information Network); union catalogs (the National Union Catalog, followed by the OCLC and RLIN databases); cooperative acquisition (the Farmington Plan); cooperative storage (the Center for Research Libraries); resource sharing (the national interlibrary loan system followed by OCLC and the Research Libraries Group applications); and a number of regional and statewide systems, which have been based upon the capabilities of some of the national developments.

There has been a distinct cyclic quality to this development, with spurts of activity interspersed by dormant periods. This has perhaps been most visible in the period since World War II, which began with a burst of research library cooperation (1945–1950, when the United States Book Exchange, the Farmington Plan, the Center for Research Libraries, and the PL-480 programs were all implemented), followed by fifteen years of inactivity (1951–1965), which was followed in turn by a decade of intense activity (1966–1976, when MARC, OCLC, RLG, and a number of regional cooperative efforts were begun). The period since 1976 has not been characterized by significant new cooperative developments.

Observing the history of research library cooperation over the last one hundred years, it is perhaps possible to draw a few conclusions. First, cooperative efforts seem to flourish most during periods of financial stress and difficulty. In the late nineteenth century, research librarians were concerned about their ability to respond to a rapid growth of the scholarly record according to their well-established modes. They proposed a variety of changes, some of them quite radical, and implemented some of those that were more conservative. In the mid-twentieth century, following the second world war, there was a second period of crisis. Scholarship was once again expanding at a rapid rate, and research librarians were again concerned about their ability to maintain pace. The proposed changes were generally less radical than those urged earlier, and more were implemented. Since that time, the pendulum has swung at a much more rapid rate. Brief periods of affluence and cooperative inactivity have alternated with equally brief periods of retrenchment and cooperative expansion. It is easy to conclude from this that research library cooperation can only proceed during threatening times. Indeed, there seems to be a good deal of justification for such a conclusion.

It is even more important, however, to recognize that there are limits to both the amount and the kind of research library cooperation that have been possible. The dismal results of efforts to pursue cooperative collection development are particularly illustrative. Given the nature of the print record and the difficulties of securing needed items quickly and effectively from distant locations, it has been incumbent upon research librarians to emphasize local collection development priorities. As a consequence, cooperative efforts in these areas have continued to exist only at the margin, focusing upon the more esoteric materials that will elicit little if any demand. It is rather indicative, for example, that less than 1 percent of research library circulation is via interlibrary loan.

At the same time, important issues have been raised in the discussions of cooperation that have proceeded during the past century—issues that have a particular resonance for research librarians as they move into the electronic era. This is especially true with respect to the notion of a library of record: a single, comprehensive, generally available collection that comprises all recorded scholarship. This ideal has never been completely abandoned in one hundred years of cooperative development. Largely ignored, and certainly honored primarily in the breach, it remains a cloudy and distant grail, vaguely hovering in the background of research library cooperative efforts.

At one point, during the 1970s, this concept took flesh and was put forward as a serious proposal, in the form of a National Periodicals Center. Although the plan for a such a center never assumed the full trappings of a comprehensive library of record, it incorporated many of the essential features of such a library. Modeled on the British Library Lending Division, it was proposed that a center be established to acquire the core periodical literature, making it available, on demand, to libraries in the form of photocopy. Several benefits were identified, including reducing the interlibrary lending burden of research libraries, reducing the acquisition burden of many libraries, improving preservation prospects, and establishing a basis for further cooperative endeavors.

Supported by a number of respected research library spokespersons and influential research library organizations, the plan, which included a request for federal funding, initially elicited important governmental interest. In spite of this momentum, and perhaps also because of it, opposition to the proposed center rose gradually in several quarters. Opponents included publishers, members of the information industry, and public librarians, as well as a number of research librarians. Specific objections included the Center's governance structure, its preservation and sale functions, its academic library emphasis, and its threat to regional interlibrary resource-sharing arrangements.

Lingering in the background, through all of the debate, was the specter of a single comprehensive research library serials collection, which could, in whole or in part, potentially replace the collections of individual research libraries. When the chips were down, few research librarians were willing to support a plan which placed primary responsibility for acquisition and maintenance of core journals—in many respects, the most essential part of the scholarly record—in the hands of an external, collaborative entity. Consequently, the early research librarian consensus evaporated, and the effort failed.

During the course of the debate, proponents revived another research library cooperative concept that had surfaced earlier, been discussed with some vigor, and then largely forgotten or at least ignored. This was the idea that research library cooperation should be clustered around a small number of regional centers, each of which would be a particularly distinctive research library. As proposed during the center debate, this concept was an obvious compromise, intended to reassure the largest and most influential research libraries that they would have a major place —indeed, *the* major place—in a cooperative effort.

This proposal had failed originally, and it failed again as a device to gather and hold needed support for the National Periodicals Center proposal. As is often the case with compromises, it did not gain the active support of its target audience and it lost further support in other quarters. In this instance, it alienated librarians in a number of research libraries who feared a definitive demarcation between "elite" and other libraries, an issue that has long been a hindrance to the growth of research library cooperation. Ultimately, consideration of the Center proposal dwindled into factional squabbling and Congress took no action.

Postmortem reviews of the Center proposal have suggested various reasons for its demise; however, everyone has agreed that no central issue was put forward that attracted and retained the necessary consensus, particularly among research librarians. This may well be because the most fundamental issue was never laid upon the table. This is, of course, the long-term need for and desirability of a single, comprehensive collection that could approximate, as closely as possible, the entire record of scholarship. Rather, the proposal was explicitly designed to address some urgent but certainly secondary research library issues: acquisition pressures related to serials and increases in interlibrary loan burdens.

It was also advocated as a redirection from institutional to collaborative objectives, whereby research librarians would begin to redirect their energies from local concerns toward the concern that they all shared, common support for scholarship. What was never adequately recognized was that research libraries are, *de facto*, engaged in a collaborative activity—maintenance of the scholarly record—which they continue to pursue with very little actual collaboration.

Previous research library cooperative programs had not provided the necessary basis on which to build a proposal that was as radical as the establishment of a National Periodicals Center. Each of these programs—from the provision of LC printed cards through MARC to OCLC and RLG; from the Farmington Plan through the Center for Research Libraries to the National Program for Acquisition and Cataloging—was scrupulous in maintaining its focus on strengthening the individual library. None of them sought to replace local emphasis with a collaborative effort, particularly one whose basis was a common, rather than an individual, objective. Within a tradition that had always pursued its shared purpose through individual initiatives, such a change in approach was revolutionary and threatening. Consequently, it was put forward tentatively and inexplicitly, and it was quickly modified under pressure.

On the other hand, it is unlikely that a more radical proposal could have been justified at the time. In this connection, it is useful to examine one particular argument that surfaced during the debate. This is the contention, advanced primarily by members of the information industry, that the proposal was fundamentally flawed by its emphasis on print collections, which, in turn, led to reliance upon photocopy and mail transmission. Noting that printing was increasingly being done from electronic data, it was argued that any program of this magnitude should be built around the use of these data and should involve electronic storage and transmission.

This criticism did, in fact, identify the major failing of the Center proposal: that it outfitted a plan suitable for an electronic information environment in the trappings of the print era. Unfortunately, the practicality of an electronic-technology-based approach was simply not demonstrable even 10 years ago, nor was the speed with which such practicality could be achieved.

Conversely, a centralized print collection offers few significant benefits in any era. The experience of the British Library Lending Division has shown that a central collection, using photocopy and mail transport, can improve access to print materials; however, because of the cost and difficulties involved in sharing these materials, the dimension of improvement is, at best, merely additive. It does not free research libraries from the need to acquire, catalog, and maintain as much of the scholarly record as they can manage.

Nor, in the final analysis, do research librarians wish to be freed from these responsibilities in a print environment. Their objective remains to build, organize, and preserve their particular collections. A major shift toward collaborative effort, focused upon the core journals that comprise the heart of the scholarly record and utilizing mechanisms that have only served peripherally in the past, has few attractions. It is no wonder that, in the final analysis, most research librarians preferred to lobby for continued federal support in the form of subsidy for local collection development rather than the establishment of a new, duplicative common collection.

It is, however, unfortunate that the original Center proposal was not more explicitly forward-looking when first presented and that it was so heavily diluted and qualified in the course of subsequent debate. The time was, in many ways, particularly ripe for a broad and serious discussion of the research library's future. The new electronic technology was emerging, having its initial impact in visible areas. The burden of maintaining the status quo in research libraries—confronted by increasing rates of print publication, rapidly mounting inflation, and reduced funding—was perceived as critical. Cooperative programs were expanding.

Proposal of a radically collaborative approach to preservation and maintenance of the scholarly record, built upon the new electronic technology, would have been advantageous in several ways. It would have broadened discussion of the future of the research library and of research library cooperation. It would have provided a more enlightened context for development of individual and cooperative library planning. It would have helped research librarians to focus, at a very critical time, on the most fundamental and significant issue confronting them: how best to fulfill their historic responsibility in the developing electronic environment.

Unfortunately, this issue receded further and further into the background during the Center debate; and, since the collapse of the Center proposal, local issues have once again dominated research librarians' agendas. Much effort has been invested in competitive programs and in divisive struggles, such as copyright of databases. Research librarians have concentrated on institutional concerns, and even the limited current cooperative programs, both regional and national, are threatened.

It is, in fact, quite ironic that the new technology, which can, for the first time in their history, provide the basis for a truly collaborative effort on the part of research librarians, is presently being applied in ways that seem to diminish the need for even the limited cooperation that has recently existed. Bibliographic data, previously available only from central data banks, is being copied and distributed on disk, eliminating certain kinds of cost and dependency, but also reducing the benefits of collaborative database creation and its ability to support expanded collection sharing. Just as technology begins to offer research librarians the opportunity to free themselves from their historic burden of redundant maintenance of the scholarly record through collaboration, many librarians seem to be searching for ways to disentangle themselves from even their present, limited cooperative alliances. In the past, short-term pressures have generally driven research library cooperative efforts, just as local objectives have constrained them. This has, perhaps, been inevitable in an era in which technology severely limited the scope of cooperation. With the rise of the new technology, this is no longer the case. Long-term considerations must now prevail, as research librarians move closer and closer to the most critical choice in their history, between gradual dissolution of the scholarly record or achievement of its long-sought but never-accomplished completion. It is essential that the leaders of the research library community recognize the importance of the decision that lies before them and galvanize movement to fulfill the research librarian's shared responsibility in a collaborative mode.

One final, particularly important practical lesson is, perhaps, evident in the failure of the National Periodicals Center effort. This is the need for research librarians to pursue their common objectives with a high degree of consensus and commitment. Differences among research librarians, attempts to cover too broad a spectrum of varied library interests, incorporation of extraneous divisive issues, lack of sufficient time and effort invested in reaching agreement—all of these shortcomings were visible in the struggle over the National Periodicals Center. Such strategies will not meet the far greater challenge that lies ahead.

5

Directing Change

Librarians must be more willing not just to accept change, but to become its agents.

Frederick G. Kilgour

The solutions of our research library problems are not to be found in Washington, but in the voluntary and concerted actions of a peer group of research libraries with a common need and a common interest in solving those problems.

Richard DeGennaro

Although the new information storage and communication technology of the electronic era has the capability to provide for a complete, fully controlled record of scholarship, there is no certainty that this will, in fact, occur. On the contrary, there is much to suggest that, rather than solving the scholarly record's longstanding shortcomings, the new technology will be applied in ways that increase the problems of managing and using scholarly information. The result will depend upon how the new technology is applied and, to a considerable extent, upon who directs this application.

Whatever else happens, scholarly communication will certainly be profoundly changed by the new technology. Such change may be largely directed, or it may be, substantially or even entirely, undirected. If it is to be directed toward achieving a complete and controlled scholarly record, the research librarian is uniquely suited to provide essential leadership in charting this new direction.

Given the complex institutional setting of the research library, as well as the number of parties interested in the state of the record of scholarship, this will not be a particularly easy or casual undertaking. If handled appropriately, however, it will have an outstanding chance of succeeding. There are two reasons for this. First, the research librarian is in the best position to understand the critical issues involved and how to deal with them. Second, the change will be demonstrably beneficial to each of the principle interested parties.

The new electronic technology is influencing scholarly communication, just as it is influencing communication in all other sectors of society. Scholars are interacting with each other via electronic mail. Scholarly publishers are experimenting with various forms of electronic publication, including electronic journals. Increasing amounts of government publication are available in electronic form. Drafts of papers are being distributed electronically before they are prepared and submitted for print publication in scholarly journals. Reports and other materials not intended for formal publication are being more widely distributed than in the past because of the new technology.

Much of this communication is using devices that are simply extending the capabilities of print. This is particularly the case with facsimile transmission, but it is also characteristic of the distribution of information on read-only compact disc. In both instances, electronic media are used, like print, to dispense information packaged in multiple copies, thereby ignoring its capabilities to provide widespread access to a single copy. In other instances, however, the latter model is being utilized for an increasing amount of scholarly information or information of scholarly value, including bibliographic data as well as full text.

Clearly, all of these developments are going to proceed. It seems most likely that there is going to be, at the very least, a gradual increase in electronic scholarly publication. Some publication may be distributed electronically rather than in print; some electronic publication may simply be an added alternative to present print publication. As scholars become more used to and involved in electronic text transmission, they will become more comfortable with and interested in extending its use further into even the most standard, core areas of scholarly publication.

Such a vision of the future is, of course, quite familiar to research librarians, who are now well acquainted with a number of electronic applications, such as online bibliographic databases, online catalogs, an increasing volume of electronic government publication, and the rapidly growing marketing of CD-ROM. One view is that electronic formats will simply be incorporated into the research library, side by side with print. The research library will modify its activities to accommodate this new form, but will continue to operate largely in its present mode. In this view, print is seen to be the dominant form of scholarly communication through the foreseeable future. It is assumed that research librarians will adapt to whatever changes emerge.

An alternative perspective anticipates much more rapid growth of electronic scholarly communication, and, indeed, expresses concern that more and more of this communication is likely to bypass the library. Advocates of this view urge research librarians to ally themselves with others interested in electronic communication, such as university computing and/or data processing centers, in order to ensure their prominence within the new electronic information environment.

A third view is that electronics will soon replace print as the preferred mode of all scholarly communication, including publication. Its exponents anticipate that libraries will no longer be needed in an electronic information environment, and that research libraries will gradually decline to a museum-like role, housing old and increasingly little-used print collections. This view tends to be aligned with perceptions of futurists regarding patterns of social change, of which scholarly communication is only one part.

For many futurists, technological advance is making possible a return to a "cottage industry" mode of social and economic activity. They perceive information users assembling personal information stores from a wide variety of electronic sources without leaving their workplaces. They anticipate a rather rapid shift from print to electronics on the part of most information producers, thus making electronic access the preferred information-seeking mode.

There are some rather significant problems with each of these models of natural or undirected evolution into the electronic information environment. The gradual mode does not seem to recognize the full potential of the new technological capabilities. Consequently, it is suspect for being unrealistic as well as conservative.

Advocates of alliances between research librarians and those already engaged in electronic communication appear to be reacting to both the glamour and the potential threat of the new mode, without adequate attention to the librarian's historic role and how this will be affected by the new technology. They generally assume that the librarian will continue the traditional print information maintenance role, with all of the effort that requires, while at the same time assuming new but not clearly defined responsibilities for a broad range of electronic information.

The futurists, in their fully justified enthusiasm for the new technology, tend to confuse access convenience with the rather different convenience that scholars seek. Exponents of this point of view recognize the need for organizing the deluge of information that scholars will have available at their fingertips, assuming that they can identify and locate its sources. They suggest that such organization can be provided if each scholar creates his or her own index.

Of course, the ready availability of vast amounts of unorganized information is not what scholars want; nor do they want to organize this information. Convenience, for scholars, means being able to secure precisely the information they need and no more, and to devote as little time as possible to information-seeking and organizing.

This is the fundamental problem with any undirected shift from a print to an electronic mode for the distribution of scholarly information. Whether the transition is brief or prolonged, extensive or relatively limited, the result will be an increase in the amount and complexity of information available to the scholar. Such a result is likely to be more of a burden than a benefit. The attractions of ready access to enormous electronic stores of information must be balanced against the threat of increased overload that such action will bring. At the very least, quantities of unused information in a variety of data stores will join, or perhaps replace, the unused print collections in research libraries. Similarly, unread text in scholars' own electronic data stores will be as neglected as the unread journals collecting dust on their office shelves.

Finally, and perhaps most important, if scholarly communication's transition to an electronic information era is undirected and piecemeal, both the research library and the record of scholarship, which it houses and maintains, are potentially threatened with extinction. It has been suggested that the research library can, and should, survive as a kind of electronic switching center, linking the scholar with many different information stores located around the world. The logistics of such a vision are unimaginably complex. How will needed information be identified and located in such a system? How will access be achieved? Where will one turn for ultimate recourse? How and by whom will this disparate array of information be validated? It is a vision of chaos—the very chaos that the structure of the scholarly record, preserved by research librarians in research libraries, presently prevents.

The prospects of such chaos in an electronic information environment have already been recognized by scholars and scholarly publishers, the research librarians' major partners in the scholarly communication process. Publishers' concerns are substantial. They worry about the loss of authentication and control. They worry about information overload. They worry about maintaining the integrity of the communication process. They anticipate disorder, perhaps developing into anarchy.

Research librarians can and should take the lead in addressing this crisis. They are uniquely suited to do so. They understand the organization and structure of the scholarly record. They can design and implement a plan for its continued maintenance in the electronic era. Furthermore, recognizing the era's capabilities, they can develop a plan that will not simply maintain the scattered, incomplete, redundant record of the past and present, but will produce a much more complete and better organized record in the future.

In doing this, it will be necessary for research librarians, first of all, to achieve understanding, consensus, and commitment within their own community—among research librarians generally. This will take considerable time and effort. It must be approached deliberately. A viable plan for consolidating, indexing, and providing general access to a scholarly record in electronic form will require considerable study, analysis, discussion, and negotiation. Because such a plan will certainly involve major and fundamental changes in the nature of the research library and in the functions of the research librarian, extended negotiation will be essential in order to reach effective consensus.

Once consensus has been achieved among research librarians, it will be important to enlist the understanding and support of other primary interested parties. The research librarian functions within a complex institutional setting. This setting includes research universities, higher education organizations, scholarly organizations, scholarly publishers and their organizations, other kinds of libraries, library organizations, and librarians' organizations. A significant change in the research library will be of more than passing interest to all of these groups.

It will, however, require the active participation of only two: the scholar and the scholarly publisher. Each will be increasingly predisposed to a reshaping of scholarly communication processes because of problems that they are increasingly confronting. For the scholar, these will be the disorder and overload of proliferating, unstructured communication. The scholarly publisher's primary concern will be loss of control of the publication process. They will share a common concern for maintenance of peer review and authentication of works of scholarship. They both recognize that it is essential to preserve the scholarly record.

Despite genuine and deep-seated concerns, it is probable that scholars will look to the librarian and publisher to take primary responsibility for planning and implementing the change. Just as they wish to spend no more time than is necessary in utilizing the scholarly record, scholars will not wish to invest significant time or effort in the actual work of changing it. At the same time, scholars will need to be assured—and perhaps frequently reassured—that these changes will be beneficial and, above all, that the record will be preserved.

The scholarly publisher will certainly want to be heavily involved in plans and decisions related to publication practices, particularly those involved in editorial judgments and the distribution of scholarly products. Recognizing that such publication has been and continues to be subsidized, largely through research library subscriptions, the publisher will want to ensure that there is continued adequate financial support for publication in whatever redesign emerges. Because scholarly publishers are directly linked to scholars through the scholarly societies and universities in which they are situated and through the editorial boards and reviewers who advise them, their primary concerns will be those that they share with scholars: the continued health and vitality of the scholarly communication process and preservation of the scholarly record.

A plan that will maintain the viability of the record of scholarship as a means of validating scholars' contributions, of documenting editorial decisions, and of providing ultimate access to scholarly products will meet the requirements of scholars and scholarly publishers in the future. If, in addition, it can offer the scholar improved convenience and reliability, it will be particularly attractive. This, in fact, should be the goal of research librarians in the electronic era.

Creation of a complete, unified electronic record of scholarship will, of course, achieve this. Completing and unifying the record in electronic form will be a monumental task. It will require a great deal of effort on the part of research librarians, sustained over a considerable period of time. Furthermore, its accomplishment will fundamentally transform not only the research library but also the role and responsibilities of the research librarian.

This change is likely to occur in two stages. First, it will be essential to unify, complete, and fully index the scholarly record. This will require the highest level of concerted effort on the part of research librarians of any activity undertaken during the entire change process. It will also demand the agreement, support, and cooperation of scholarly publishers—the societies and universities who, together, produce much of the scholarly record and most of its "core" literature.

The second stage will involve the reconfiguration of the research library and of the role of the research librarian. This will necessarily be carried out within each library. Here, also, the research librarians will have to undertake the major effort, working with their respective scholarly communities and campus administrations, probably through appropriate institutional structures such as library committees and deans' councils.

In each of these stages, it will be essential for research librarians to frame the issues, identify solutions, design and implement model programs, negotiate agreements—in brief, to perform effectively all of the leadership functions necessary to achieve change in a complex environment. Librarians will need to take the initiative with the other major parties in order to ensure the most productive result. They will also have to identify in advance and focus upon the benefits that will accrue to the other participants.

Of course, most people are unwilling to give up present benefits in exchange for offered, but undelivered, future improvements. This will certainly be the case with scholars and scholarly publishers. They will not abandon present practices in exchange for a newly designed system until they are convinced that the resulting system will be an improvement over what they presently have. It will be the research librarian's responsibility to demonstrate the value of the new mode before the old one is discarded.

This will mean that the present research library must be maintained and operated at the same time that its replacement is being established. Print collections will not be forsaken until electronic access is available, tested, and found to be satisfactory. Traditional services cannot be eliminated before the newer and better services are provided. This is, of course, one of the most challenging aspects of institutional change.

Change of this dimension will not arrive overnight. On the contrary, it will certainly require several decades of concerted, coordinated effort, probably extending over more than the working life of a single generation. Throughout this transition, research librarians must preserve necessary consensus, both among themselves and with their scholar and scholarly publisher colleagues, in order to bring the entire process to successful closure.

If research librarians respond effectively to these challenges, however, they should be able to reshape the record of scholarship as well as the organization and function of the research library to conform to the requirements of the new electronic information environment.

6

Controlled Completeness: Consolidating the Record of Scholarship

Books were once the available technology for the transmission of ideas across time and space. Library buildings were once seen as means of protecting books from piracy and other dangers. The difficulty with structures invented to serve purposes at one point in time is that they live beyond their function. Soon, systems feel constrained to define their functions in terms of the available structures, forgetting that structures are inventions.

Brenda Dervin

Creation of a single, unified electronic record of scholarship will satisfy, for the first time in their history, research librarians' quest for completeness. Creation of a comprehensive bibliographic apparatus for this record will fulfill, also for the first time, research librarians' efforts to establish control over the record.

To achieve completeness, the research librarian will have to gather together, or arrange to have gathered, an electronic record containing all extant scholarly publications, past, present, and future. It will include material in all languages. It will cover all scholarly disciplines. It will contain items which were originally issued in a variety of formats.

To achieve control, the research librarian will have to organize this record so that each distinguishable bit of information it contains can be identified and retrieved at need. This will require the creation and maintenance of a comprehensive and highly specific index, covering the entire contents of the record. To house and maintain the record and its apparatus, it will be necessary to establish a center for the electronic record of scholarship, with adequate connections to the entire scholarly community.

A complete record of scholarship necessarily includes all reports of scholarly inquiry. It must cover all disciplines, specialties, and sub-specialties. It must encompass all languages. It must contain all forms, such as monographs, journals, reports, and proceedings, as well as more ephemeral materials. It must embrace not only all current records, but all that exist from the past as well. It must also provide for assembling and incorporating all future scholarly products.

The contents of a fully controlled scholarly record must be completely and specifically identified. It is not sufficient to catalog and provide subject control over each of the incorporated works. A detailed index, identifying each meaningful component of the entire record, must be provided. Functioning like the index to a single monograph or journal volume, this comprehensive index must identify each salient reference in every work and, consequently, in the entire record. Furthermore, it must effectively relate that reference to other similar references, throughout the record. It must go beyond this to link various groups of related references to each other. Finally, it must link each individual reference to the work in which it appeared.

Thus, the bibliographic apparatus will need to incorporate the most important features of both the index and the catalog. It will provide the detail and relationships of the former without sacrificing the identification provided by the latter. It will enable a user to search comprehensively at the index level, irrespective of the particular works involved, and also to distinguish any and all works, including author, date, and publisher, as desired.

The most essential material to incorporate into the electronic scholarly record will be the core scholarly publications, the refereed journals produced by learned societies and the refereed monographs from university presses. This material comprises the most respected and most used portion of the record. Its incorporation can be accomplished through agreement with the publishers.

Electronic copy is now produced for all of this material, as part of the printing process. Arrangements need to be worked out to gather this copy and integrate it, as the beginning of the electronic record. This copy will include the indexes for all of this material, which can form the basis of the electronic apparatus. To this it will be necessary to add catalog copy for each of the works, which is presently being generated as part of the publication process.

Using this data, research librarians and systems experts can begin to design the electronic record and its bibliographic apparatus. This design will include an index structure and vocabulary. When the design is finished, the database can be enlarged to include other segments of the record. Also, once the initial design is completed and implemented, trial access can be provided to the nation's research libraries, so as to begin to test communication and use factors.

Remaining components of the scholarly record include research reports, conference proceedings, government publications, drafts and other fugitive materials, and commercial publications. Some of this material exists only in print form, some exists only in electronic form, and some is presently in both formats. Technically, it will probably be easier to incorporate the electronic materials first; however, there are other considerations that will certainly influence the sequencing.

Research reports and conference proceedings are presently among the most sought-after and difficult-to-obtain portions of the scholarly record. Few research libraries presently acquire available print copies because of the cost and complication involved in identifying, locating, and securing these items. Incorporation of this material into the electronic record will be extremely valuable to the scholarly community. As with the core monographs and journals, electronic copies of much of this material should be available for inclusion in the record.

Fugitive material, the so-called "gray literature," represents a somewhat different challenge. As electronic information storage and communication is more widely used by the scholarly community, an increasing amount of this material is appearing in electronic form. Furthermore, the convenience of electronic communication is causing this material to proliferate. It includes research findings, commentary, and similar preliminary or ephemeral scholarly products. This material poses an increasingly difficult problem for the scholarly community, both because of the irregularity of its distribution and because its value is not validated through the referee process. Its limited and often selective circulation together with its unreliable and often nonexistent bibliographic coverage gives it a kind of shadow status within the spectrum of scholarly information. Its incorporation into the electronic record and apparatus will be of substantial benefit to the scholarly community.

The availability of a central electronic scholarly record will provide opportunity to gather and organize this material. A simple electronic code can easily distinguish this and other non-refereed segments of the record from those that have passed peer review. In the absence of a central record, gathering and organizing this material will pose increasingly difficult problems. Such a task is now and will continue to be beyond the capability of any single library. With the creation of a central scholarly record, recognized by the scholarly community as the authoritative record of scholarship, this situation could be completely transformed. Responsibility for including fugitive items in the record could be lodged entirely with their authors or producers. If they wished their products to receive attention and recognition—in short, to be acknowledged as part of the record of scholarship—it would be their responsibility to provide electronic copy for such inclusion. In effect, a complete, consolidated scholarly record could function as a depository for all recorded information deemed to have scholarly value.

More and more government publications, many of which incorporate important scholarly information, are appearing exclusively in electronic form. This material will have to be added to the electronic record, as will the electronic versions—also available as a byproduct of the present printing process—of governmental print publications.

Finally, it will be important for the electronic record to contain a substantial amount of commercial publication. Appropriate arrangements will have to be worked out with publishers to ensure that the accessibility of this material in the electronic record does not adversely affect the sale of their print products. A variety of options are available to accomplish this, some of which have already been tested.

Once arrangements such as these have been achieved, incorporation of all present and future works of scholarship in the electronic record will be assured. As these arrangements are being negotiated and implemented, it will be essential for research librarians to undertake a coordinated effort to convert the present print record to electronic form, so as to complete the electronic record.

Major portions of the world's research library print collections are presently in immediate or near-term jeopardy. Because of the chemical nature of the paper on which they are printed, millions of volumes are either presently unusable or are rapidly approaching that point. An increasing number of print volumes have, in fact, deteriorated to the point of being irrecoverable. A variety of efforts have been undertaken to deal with this problem. These include several kinds of chemical treatments as well as replacement through filming. Because of costs and other difficulties associated with alternative means, research librarians have largely settled on microfilming as the most viable long-term remedy. A significant number of research libraries now have active microfilm-preservation programs, and major national research library organizations are engaged in planning and fund raising efforts to implement a coordinated national program.

One of the central goals of such a program will certainly be to avoid unnecessary duplication, and thereby maximize the use of available resources, by microfilming no more than one copy of each distinctive item. Under such an arrangement, the library holding the first microfilm copy will be obliged to provide a positive version of its copy to other libraries on demand. To further these endeavors, a national bibliographic database, identifying microform copies, has been established.

This is an expensive program, which, unfortunately, is tied to the technology of the print era. Of all formats developed to package information during this era, microform is undoubtedly the most unpopular with scholars. It is, in a variety of ways, much less convenient to use than the book. Because of its dependence on print reproduction, the preservation program ties microform to interlibrary loan, another research library activity that generally ranks low with the users of research libraries.

Despite these shortcomings, microfilming has clearly seemed to be the most cost-effective solution available to meet the deterioration of research library print collections. This is no longer the case, particularly recognizing that preservation is a major worldwide problem and that its solution will necessarily extend far into the future, probably as far as anyone can presently see and certainly well into the electronic era.

Massive microfilming of research library collections will, perhaps more than any other step that research librarians can take, strengthen their ties to the past and complicate their progress into the future. It will ensure that the vast majority of their retrospective collections remains in a print format, with all of the problems that this will entail in an electronic environment. Finally and most importantly, it will risk the long-term and perhaps permanent division of the scholarly record into print and electronic components, thus forestalling creation of a complete, consolidated electronic record. This is particularly unfortunate, because the alternative of converting these materials to electronic form is perhaps the most important single effort that research librarians can presently make toward achieving ultimate completion of the record of scholarship.

The technology is presently available to accomplish such conversion, and improvements are continuing to be made. A decision by the research library community to abandon its various print preservation programs and redirect its efforts toward electronic conversion would enable it to stimulate further improvements in conversion technology.

Clearly, substantial funding is going to be generated to preserve the deteriorating portions of the print scholarly record. Investment of these funds in electronic conversion would provide great impetus to creation of a complete electronic record. It would also improve the general accessibility of the preserved portions of the record; whereas, microform preservation, with its continued dispersal of holdings and its dependence upon interlibrary loan, will certainly diminish access. Finally, such an effort would position research librarians at the forefront of movement into the electronic era, rather than relegate them to continued pursuit of print solutions. No present decision by research librarians has more significance with regard to their future and the future of the scholarly record than the choice between microfilming and print-electronic conversion with respect to the preservation of deteriorated print materials.

As research librarians move forward in assembling the complete electronic record, they will also need to create an electronic bibliographic apparatus. Such an apparatus will have several major advantages over the present print apparatus. It will reduce complexity. It will provide greater specificity of coverage. It will eliminate inconsistency. Finally, it will provide complete coverage of the electronic record.

The print bibliographic apparatus has two levels. The first is an index level, which identifies the contents of works. There are a great range and variety of indexes, including indexes to individual monographs, to journal volumes, to all or most publications of particular categories, to library collections. Some of these indexes are highly specific and quite detailed. Others are broad and general.

The second level is the catalog level, which identifies and describes printed volumes, the packages in which works are produced and distributed. As with indexes, there are many different kinds of catalogs. There are catalogs of the publications of countries, of commercial publications, of publications by format, of the holdings of individual libraries, of the holdings of groups of libraries, of works on a topic, of works by a particular author.

In order to search comprehensively in the print scholarly record it is essential to use both levels of its bibliographic apparatus, moving back and forth between them. This will not be necessary with the electronic apparatus. Indexing and cataloging can be integrated in an electronic database, allowing the user to relate information about any portion of the contents of a work to information about the work itself, directly and conveniently. The electronic apparatus can, thus, provide a single level of bibliographic coverage through linkage of each bit of indexed information to the author, title, publisher, and date of the work in which it appeared.

Each index reference can also be linked to the text in question—the particular section of text to which the reference refers as well as the entire work of which that text is a part. This will provide for rapid movement from an index citation to the cited passage to the surrounding text. This integration of index and content will reduce a great deal of the complexity of the print record and its apparatus, where users, having identified desired works in catalogs and indexes, must then determine where those works are held, seek them out, and secure them, assuming their availability.

Print indexes presently provide a great range of specificity in their coverage. Indexes of individual books generally afford the greatest specificity, through their effort to identify every meaningful element of text. At the other extreme are the indexes covering many works, such as library subject catalogs or major periodical indexes, which generally restrict their coverage to the most prominent topics dealt with in each work. The specificity of the individual book index cannot be provided in more extensive print indexes because of capacity and workload limitations. Such extensive indexes are much too large and complicated to use easily, to maintain effectively, and to edit consistently.

These limitations do not apply to electronic indexes, which have the capacity to store and manipulate enormous amounts of data. An electronic index can provide very detailed and specific coverage for even a very extensive electronic database. Consequently, an electronic bibliographic apparatus can provide the same level of specificity for an electronic database, potentially covering the entire scholarly record, that a detailed printed index can provide for a printed book.

The print apparatus is riddled with inconsistency. Vocabularies vary, from index to index, from index to catalog, and among catalogs. Depth and extent of coverage differ widely. Criteria for inclusion and exclusion diverge. The various components of the apparatus cannot be used interchangeably. Each has its own rules, which, more often than not, depart significantly from those of its fellows. There are no overall standards, enforced or not, and there is little coordination.

Consistency will be implicit in a single electronic apparatus. It will have to have a standardized vocabulary. It will necessarily have a uniform depth and range of coverage. Its standards for exclusion and inclusion will inevitably be the same throughout. Not being comprised of different or divergent components, the electronic apparatus will operate entirely according to one set of rules. It will have explicit standards, identically applied.

Among the shortcomings of the print apparatus, perhaps none is more frustrating than its incompleteness. The entire apparatus is extensive, including many different types and formats among its components. Becoming acquainted with its size and variety requires much time and effort. Even when that has been done, however, there is no guarantee that every applicable item has been covered. On the contrary, because the apparatus obviously does not provide complete coverage, there is always, in any information search, the nagging concern about what may have been omitted. The construction of the print apparatus, built piecemeal upon a scattered scholarly record, can provide no assurance that everything relevant is identifiable and obtainable.

Such assurance may well be the single greatest benefit of a comprehensive bibliographic apparatus covering a complete and unified scholarly record. If the record is constructed and maintained properly, if the apparatus is created correctly, it will be the reliable source of information regarding the state of scholarship on any matter.

A reliably complete scholarly record must be, by definition, a unified, consolidated record. It can no longer, as has been the case in the past, be scattered among various locations throughout the world. It must be assembled and maintained in a single location (although copies could certainly be distributed), from where it provides electronic access to the worldwide scholarly community.

The bibliographic apparatus must also be consolidated, and it must be located with the record. Indeed, the interaction between the record and its apparatus will necessarily be so close as to be inextricable. Either will, essentially, be useless without the other.

Maintenance of both the record and the apparatus will have to be performed where they are located. The activities related to gathering scholarly information and adding it to the record, monitoring the record's preservation, extending the bibliographic apparatus, overseeing the operation of the record and its access system, assisting with use of the record—all of these functions will have to be handled on site.

Thus, a center or archive will have to be established to house the record and apparatus. This center will have to be equipped, and this equipment will have to be monitored, maintained, and, as necessary, improved. It will have to be adequately staffed. Beyond personnel to oversee equipment operation and maintenance, the staff will be composed primarily of research librarians. These librarians will be responsible for extending the bibliographic apparatus, to include all additions to the record, as well as for assisting with its use.

Once all retrospective and current scholarly records are incorporated into the consolidated database and covered by its bibliographic apparatus, the long-sought objectives of the research librarian will have been achieved. The record of scholarship will have been completed and fully controlled. This accomplishment should, in turn, make it possible to provide the scholar with what he has sought for so long: convenience and reliability in his search for information about the state of scholarship on any matter.

Clearly, a complete and fully controlled scholarly record is a prerequisite to convenient and reliable access to that record by the scholarly community. However, will such a record, in and of itself, be sufficient to guarantee those desired results? The answer to this question is central to understanding the nature and characteristics of the future research library.

7

Reliable Convenience: The Future Research Library

If the typical instrument of descriptive control is the exhaustive national or subject bibliography, perhaps the typical means of exploitative control would be the "special" library serving a group of scholars accustomed to talking to each other, and staffed by persons approaching the type of the bibliographical consultant rather than the bibliographical aide.

Patrick Wilson

A move toward electronic media is simultaneously a move toward interactive use.

A. J. Meadows

Creation of a complete, consolidated, fully organized and controlled electronic record of scholarship, readily available to scholars everywhere, should, at long last, respond fully to the scholar's requirement for convenient and reliable access to needed information regarding the state of scholarship on any topic. Unfortunately, this is not the case. Use of the bibliographic apparatus, the necessary means of access to the record, by anyone not well versed in its structure and vocabulary, will not meet the standard of reliability.

As a consequence, scholars will have to depend upon the research librarian, the expert in the bibliographic apparatus and its use, to act as intermediary. This new role will augment and extend the librarian's primary historical role, maintenance of the scholarly record. By this process, the present research library will be transformed into an information center, which, together with the center housing the record of scholarship, will comprise the future research library.

Scholars, seated at their personal computers or electronic workstations, querying the complete electronic record through the use of its bibliographical apparatus, would seem, finally, to have achieved convenient and reliable access to the record of scholarship. No longer will they have to struggle through a welter of bibliographic sources. No longer will they have to move back and forth between indexes and catalogs in order to determine what they need and where it is located. No longer will they have to be concerned about the availability of the item or items they need. No longer need they worry about the possible existence of information that they cannot locate.

Rather, scholars will simply forward their requests electronically, review proffered citations, browse as they wish in the relevant text of cited works, and call up or even print out any data they need.

If they so wish, they can broaden their search into identified related topics. If they need to pursue a citation trail, they can do so electronically. If they want information about a particular author, it will be provided. At any point in the search, they can change direction, following a reference or an entire line of inquiry they have chanced upon. Throughout the entire search, scholars will have available, literally at their fingertips, the total information resource of the scholarly record.

Such information searching could hardly be more convenient. Assuming the availability of equipment, it could be done anywhere—at home, in an office or laboratory. It could be done at any time, when an idea strikes or in intervals between other research activities. Not only would such searching be superior to the use of print libraries, it would also require less effort than pursuing the scholar's present alternative channels, although these would certainly still be available.

There is only one problem: the index terminology and structure. Whatever index is developed to control the scholarly record will, inevitably, be idiosyncratic. This is the nature of indexes. It is imbedded in the psychology of information seeking and use. Each individual approaches information from his or her own perspective, applying his or her own terms, which are often quite different from those used by others in framing their information needs.

Of course, this does not mean that there are no common definitions. Common definitions are a necessary element in all social activity, where shared understanding of a minimum vocabulary is essential for every functioning member. It is possible for everyone active in society to retain an understanding of the common social vocabulary, because it is constantly reinforced as it is employed. Indeed, modifications in this vocabulary are not disruptive for the same reason. They are absorbed through use, a process that is sometimes observed and noticed with interest, as changes in the meanings of words take place.

Similarly, one of the salient characteristics of social sub-groups, as they distinguish themselves from the rest of society, is the development and use of distinctive vocabularies. An important element of entry into such a group is understanding the particular meanings of their terms. Regular practice and intercommunication within the group maintain a common understanding of these definitions, including whatever changes may occur.

Effective use of a common vocabulary can also be lost to those who cease to use the terms regularly. Such loss is evident in individuals who withdraw from interaction with society as a whole or with any of its groups. The ability to communicate disappears. Re-entry can be difficult and time-consuming, as much effort must be invested in relearning and learning anew the largely forgotten and inevitably changed terminology.

Every scholarly discipline comprises such a subgroup, with a distinctive set of terms to communicate its concepts. Learning this vocabulary is part of scholars' acculturation to their fields. Using it is essential to participation in their fields. Inactive scholars or former students, who decrease or abandon activity in their fields, gradually lose command of these specialized vocabularies.

So that their work is understood and appreciated by their colleagues, scholars use their discipline's unique language in all communications within their fields, including their contributions to the record of scholarship. The scholarly record is, thus, written in a great number of specialized and distinctive vocabularies. One of the problems that research librarians have traditionally confronted, in their efforts to index their collections by subject, is how to master and keep abreast of the many, constantly changing disciplinary languages—how, in effect, to regularize and unify the scholarly Tower of Babel. Despite considerable effort, this has proved to be a fruitless undertaking. What librarians have succeeded in doing is devising yet another specialized vocabulary, a vocabulary that is essentially their own.

Of course, there was no other way to index the scholarly record. It would be literally impossible for research librarians to immerse themselves sufficiently in the entire spectrum of scholarly specialties so as to produce and maintain a vocabulary that reflected them all. Moreover, the resulting vocabulary would be so technical that it would be fully useful only in parts, to the specialists who understood those particular terminologies. Given the research librarian's self-service posture, which has assumed that any index or catalog must be widely understood by its users, conscious effort has been, and continues to be, made to translate esoteric terms into those that are more generally recognizable.

This has not succeeded either. The librarian's terminology remains yet another specialized terminology, which members of the scholarly community have neither the time nor the inclination to learn. The disparity between librarians' definitions and those of the various specialties is one of the major problems that characterize the print bibliographic apparatus. It will be no different with the electronic apparatus.

Because of the inevitable idiosyncrasy of the bibliographic apparatus' terminology, it will be very difficult for scholars to use the electronic record. If, in an information search, they do not use the correct term or terms, they may not secure precisely the information they need. If the choice of terms is precise, they may miss the desired information altogether. If the choice is general, they may be deluged with information, which may or may not include the data they need. Under any circumstances, they will never be confident that the information searching has been successful. Consequently, however convenient the electronic record may be, it will never be reliable.

Can the scholar be rescued from this dilemma? Yes, but only by the intervention of the research librarian. The librarian is in a unique position to solve the scholar's difficulties with the use of the electronic apparatus. This will not, however, be done by way of explanation. Experience with the print apparatus has shown that explanation does not work. It is not effective, for either the scholar or the librarian, for the latter to teach the former how to use the apparatus every time he or she needs information. This violates the goal of convenience, which clearly has as much importance for the scholar as reliability.

Rather, it will be essential for the research librarian to mediate between the scholarly record and its bibliographic apparatus, on the one hand, and the information-seeking scholar on the other.

Librarians are particularly suited to perform this essential function. First, as authors of the bibliographic apparatus, they understand its organization and terminology. They, alone, can work their way through its complexities and idiosyncrasies to secure reliable information from the scholarly record. Furthermore, their continued use of the apparatus maintains the currency of their understanding.

Second, research librarians are trained and knowledgeable in diagnosing information needs. Perhaps the most significant and lasting product of their approximate fifty-year experience with organized reference service is the technique of such diagnosis. Rather than use this skill to advise scholars in the methods they should pursue to discover the information they require, as has been the case in the print era, librarians will have to move from diagnosis to therapy, using their knowledge of the bibliographic apparatus not only to define scholars' information objectives, but to secure and provide to scholars precisely the information that will meet their needs.

Historically, the reference service posture of the research librarian has undergone an evolution. In the beginning, it was reactive: little was offered and a minimum was provided, and then only on request. Gradually, it became more and more active, generating a variety of ancillary services designed to enhance the scholar's ability to use the research library. In the electronic era, with its complete centralized scholarly record, the research librarian's reference service will be interactive. It will become information service. The research librarian's primary role will be intermediation between the information needs of the scholar and the information structure of the scholarly record.

Research librarians who provide this service will be able to concentrate their full energy upon it because they will be relieved of responsibility for managing and organizing the record of scholarship. Not that research librarians will no longer be involved in this activity. Quite the contrary. The librarians at the record center will, in fact, be carrying out these very tasks. This will include all of the functions that are presently executed at each research library: gathering, organizing, and maintaining the record as well as its bibliographic apparatus. It will also include the continued provision of traditional reference service, assisting the client in the use of the scholarly record. In this instance, however, the client will be the local research librarian rather than the scholar.

Center reference librarians will keep local research librarians apprised of changes and developments in the bibliographic apparatus, its structure and vocabulary. They will help local librarians to solve problems that they encounter in the course of their searching. They will, in short, have finally fulfilled the long-standing goal of traditional reference service: helping a knowledgeable user seek information in the scholarly record.

In this information-delivery environment, the research librarians will be able to resolve, finally, their long-standing conflict between preservation and use of the scholarly record. Preserved centrally, with all of the protection required for such an essential and irreplaceable database, the record will be delivered locally in the form of electronic copies, from which print copies can be made as desired. No use will interfere with any other use, nor will it jeopardize the record's preservation.

With the availability of interactive reference service, scholars will finally achieve reliable convenience in assessing the state of scholarship on any topic. They will submit a request to the local research librarian, confident that it will be pursued effectively and exhaustively. They will know that they can rely on the librarian to neither overlook relevant information nor overload them with unneeded data. They will be confident that the search will conform to parameters agreed upon, between the research librarian and themselves, before it is begun. They will place trust in the librarian's cognitive authority, not in the scholar's subject, but in use of the bibliographic apparatus.

The search will be as convenient as the scholar's direct interaction with the electronic record, described above, except that it will include one or more diagnostic sessions with the librarian. These will generally, although not necessarily, be handled electronically, probably utilizing electronic mail so as not to interrupt unduly the schedule of either party. (At the same time, it will be desirable, if not essential, for there to be some continuing personal interaction between librarians and the scholars with whom they are dealing.) The reliability provided by the librarian's intermediation will not significantly reduce the scholar's convenience.

Through this process, the local research library will be transformed into an information center. This center, together with the record center, united by their electronic connections and interacting staffs, will comprise the future research library. This library will, for the first time in the history of research libraries, provide convenient and reliable access to the complete, fully controlled record of scholarship.

With this reconfiguration of the research library, the research librarian will enter into a new relationship with the scholar. Functioning as the scholar's primary means of information regarding the state of scholarship on any matter, the research librarian will become a more active and contributing partner in the scholarly process.

Bibliographic Essay

Several works are quoted in this book—at its beginning and at the beginning of each chapter. Each of these works is listed among the references at the end of the Bibliographic Essay that follows (as are all works discussed in the text portion of the essay itself). The specific citations for the quoted passages are: Weintraub, p. 38; Ziman, pp. 103-4; Rogers and Weber, p. 1; Price, pp. 73-74; Frye, p. 17; Masuda, p. 50; Allen, p. 15; Dizard, p. 69; Zaleznik, p. 239; Kilgour, p. 5; DeGennaro, p. 79; Dervin, p. 18; Wilson, *Two Kinds of Power*, p. 150; and, Meadows, *The Future of the Printed Word*, p. 158.

THE LIBRARIAN AND INFORMATION

It is an interesting characteristic of the literature on research librarianship that it has focused on the role and functions of libraries, rather than of librarians. There is, in fact, no good current treatment of the latter topic. Consequently, one must rely upon the considerable literature on research libraries, together with some shorter treatments of particular functions, to identify what is understood in the field to be the research librarian's role.

The custodial character of this role has also not been widely discussed, perhaps because it has simply been assumed. Rothstein used the term in his 1961 discussion of academic library reference service: "Traditionally, the librarian's role . . . has been that of custodian, collector, and cataloger" (p. 12). Rogers and Weber, in what remains the standard text in the field, identify eight basic research library functions, five of which directly relate to acquiring, preserving, and maintaining collections. The other three, taken together, account for perhaps 5 percent of the average research library budget (pp. 1-3).

The crucial importance of the research library's role in preserving the scholarly record has been identified by the National Enquiry (Scholarly Communication: The Report of the National Enquiry; pp. 132-33). The literature on research library acquisition and collection development practices has generally advocated a comprehensive approach. This has been discussed at length by Osburn (Academic Research and Library Resources), who also examines the lack of coordination among libraries. Many commentators have, particularly over the last two decades, noted the impossibility of research libraries acquiring the entire compass of scholarly publication. Rogers's relatively recent comments are typical.

The library catalog's primary role as a "finding device" has been analyzed by Patrick Wilson ("The Catalog as Access Mechanism: Background and Concepts"). Library classification as knowledge classification is discussed by Davison. The continued focus of the Dewey Decimal Classification, the oldest among extant library classification schemes, is identified in the introduction to its latest edition: "In the DDC, basic classes are organized by traditional academic disciplines or fields of study. No principle is more basic to the DDC than this: the parts of the classification are arranged by discipline, not by subject" (p. xxvi). Although other classification systems have placed emphasis on relations among works according to content, rather than on fitting works into a predetermined classification of knowledge, the major differences have more to do with process than result (Needham, *Organizing Knowledge in Libraries*).

The essential contribution that research librarians have made to preserving and organizing the record of scholarship has been identified by Ziman, whose work remains authoritative in this area.

Any standard history of libraries, such as Harris's, provides discussion of the early rigorous controls applied to research library access and use, as well as their gradual relaxation over many centuries. More detail and analysis can be found in specialized studies, such as Seal's interesting and informative discussion of branch libraries.

Although there is now an extensive literature on the preservation problems of research library collections, which includes discussions of theft and vandalism, there is essentially no serious discussion of the adverse consequences of ordinary use. Practicing librarians are, however, very much aware of this dilemma. It is not discussed for the same reason that it remains a dilemma: there seems to be nothing that can be done about it.

There has been substantial discussion, in recent years, of how the complexity of research library collections and their bibliographic apparatus deter and discourage use. Osburn has observed:

> The excess of information [in research library collections] may become a serious impediment to research because of the general complexity it creates, the time required to sift through it, the general redundancies or irrelevancies of much of it, or even the idea it might foster that anything worth doing has already been done (pp. 131-32).

Both scholars (Weintraub, p. 38; Frye, p. 24) and librarians (Brittain, "Information Services and Knowledge Creation in the Social Sciences," p. 637; Stenstrom, pp. 430-31) have argued for smaller, more easily usable collections.

The librarian stereotype is treated at length and well by Pauline Wilson, who gives extensive attention to academic, although not explicitly research, librarians.

Bunge provides a brief, useful historical review of reference service, which places developments in research libraries within a national context. Halvorson's 1943 article remains a classic statement of the rationale for the self-service approach: "Those reference librarians who fail to keep the instructional function in mind in their anxiety to help the inquiring student succeed only in interfering with the intellectual development of the prospective scholar" (p. 105). That such a view remains not only active but dominant is clear from Rogers and Weber: "Too many librarians provide the factual answer or conduct the search instead of showing the reader how to do it" (p. 202). White ("The Role of Reference Service in the Mission of the Academic Library") and McClure have critiqued this approach, distinguishing between university library and special library information services. Schiller and, more recently, Nielsen have sought to reconcile or "transcend" the self-service and information-service approaches.

THE SCHOLAR AND INFORMATION

The literature on scholarly production and communication is now considerable. Several works have achieved particular authority. Ziman has described how scholarship is produced, assessed, and accepted as knowledge. Price has analyzed patterns of scholars' productivity, the growth of scholarship, and their influence on modes of scholarly communication. Crane has identified the characteristics and functions of scholars' networks.

Garvey and his colleagues at Johns Hopkins University have analyzed the scholarly communication process in detail, with particular emphasis on psychology. The National Enquiry on Scholarly Communication has analyzed this process in the humanities and social sciences, specifically focusing on the relationships among scholars, research librarians, and scholarly publishers.

In Great Britain, notable work has been done by Brittain (*Information and Its Users: A Review with Special Reference to the Social Sciences*) and Line ("The Information Uses and Needs of Social Scientists: An Overview of INFROSS") in the social sciences (Morrison); by Meadows (*Communication in Science*) in the sciences; and by Smith in the humanities. Each of these analysts has, in fact, led or been a primary participant in major investigations of scholarly communication carried out at universities: Line and Brittain at the University of Bath, Meadows at the University of Leicester, and Smith at Sheffield University. All of these investigations have given particular attention to the relationship between librarians and scholars.

In addition, a significant number of smaller, more highly focused studies have been conducted related to scholars' research methods and their use of libraries. As a consequence, a great deal is now known about scholarly practices and the contribution that research librarians make to the scholarly process.

Garvey has described the "closed" nature of scholarship's communication system, "in which information is created and processed, and then feeds back into [the system] in order to stimulate further creation and processing of information" (p. 29). Ziman (p. 103), Meadows (*Communication in Science*, p. 110), and others have noted the primacy of production over consumption in the scholar's approach to information. The selectivity of this approach has been analyzed in detail (Ziman).

The importance of reliability in scholars' information searching has been identified in the sciences (Meadows), the social sciences (Line), and the humanities (National Enquiry on Scholarly Communication). The importance that scholars attach to convenience is widely recognized. Soper found it to be the primary consideration in information searching on the part of scholars in all disciplines. Similar conclusions have been reached in separate studies covering the sciences (Meadows, pp. 124-25), the social sciences (*The Social Sciences: The Supply of and Demand for Documentation and Data*, p. 129), and the humanities (Guest, p. 165). Ziman has described the importance of convenience in the scholarly process as follows: "Without necessarily succumbing entirely to fashion, [scholars] tend to work within the conventional framework of currently received notions, and to build, opportunistically and piecemeal, upon the near and familiar work of their colleagues and contemporaries" (Ziman, p. 60).

Garvey (p. 54), Meadows (p. 92), and Frye (pp. 17-18) have all discussed the importance of priority.

Many investigators have noted the scholar's efforts, throughout history, to cope effectively with the continuously expanding store of recorded information that he, himself, produces. Price identified the scholar's sense of being "awash in a sea of . . . literature that augments in each decade as much as in all times before" (p. 13). Garvey, Frye, Brittain, Adam, and many others have discussed this problem.

Data identified in this book regarding collection use has been drawn from Bebout (pp. 40-44) for the humanities; from Roberts and Brittain (pp. 50-71) for the social sciences; and from Price (p. 67) for the sciences. The Pittsburgh study remains an important pioneering study on overall research library use, based upon analysis over an extended period of time. A number of other studies, both earlier and more recent, generally support and reinforce these findings.

Price, Garvey, Meadows, and others have discussed the clustering of citations in core journals. The figures used in this book were taken from Meadows (*Communication in Science*) in the sciences, Line (*Towards the Improvement of Social Science Information Systems*) in the social sciences, and Jones in the humanities.

Soper, whose work remains invaluable in such matters, is the source of data regarding scholars' research practices. The referenced study was carried out under the auspices of the National Enquiry.

Roberts and Brittain have stated that "it is now well known that social scientists make relatively little use of library tools and information services" (p. 50). This conclusion is supported by a number of studies, covering all disciplinary areas (*Scholarly Communication*, p. 133; Guest, p. 154; Smith, pp. 22-23; Stieg, pp. 554-56; Meadows, *Communication in Science*, p. 124; Line, "The Information Uses," p. 417; Meyriat, p. 11).

In the mid-19th century, there was a conflict between the librarian of the British Museum and scholars over cataloging the library's collection. The scholars complained that the new catalog was complex and difficult to use. A Royal Commission was appointed to resolve the matter. During its hearings, Thomas

Carlyle described the new catalog as "exceedingly inconvenient." The defense of Panizzi, the librarian, was that a simple listing of discrete works, as advocated by the scholars, was insufficient to organize the large and growing collection, whereas his new catalog categorized the works and related them to each other. Panizzi prevailed, and the collection was organized according to his system. Lubetsky, in recounting this event, concluded that Panizzi was correct and had to triumph if recorded scholarship was to be preserved in an organized state. Of course, Panizzi was correct, but so were the dissenting scholars whose ease of access was constrained.

The low rate of use of research library reference service has been documented in many different analyses, including those carried out by the National Enquiry (p. 133), Jones (p. 155), Stone (pp. 27-30), Line ("The Information Uses," p. 418), Adam (p. 338), Stenstrom (p. 429), Meadows (*Communication in Science*, p. 124), and Breton (p. 21). In relating her findings (concerning humanities scholars) to those of other investigators, Guest observed: "As an information resource, librarians were rated at the very bottom of the list by respondents which was true also in the studies of scientists, social scientists, and historians" (p. 163).

The scholars' major concerns identified in these studies related to the complexity of the library and its apparatus as well as to the fear of being overloaded with information (Katzen; Smith). This concern about information overload has been well documented (Griffith; Brittain, "Information Services"; Brittain, "Relevance of Social Science"; Meadows, *Communication in Science*; Adam; *The Social Sciences*). Garvey and Griffith have succinctly stated the problem, with respect to one discipline: "the major problem facing psychology is not so much that psychology is producing more information than its total manpower can assimilate, but rather that the individual scientist is being overloaded with scientific information" (p. 130). Roberts has discussed the scholar's overload problems resulting from research librarians providing documents rather than information. Thompson has observed that "the problem with libraries is that they can never be convenient" (p. 26).

The report of the National Enquiry noted that the research library's primary value to scholars was as a "repository" of scholarly information (*Scholarly Communication*, p. 133). The statement by Ziman, quoted at the beginning of the first chapter of this book (pp. 103-4), expresses this value extremely well. Under these circumstances, it is quite understandable that the primary complaint that scholars have about research libraries is not being able to find what they want, when they want it (*Scholarly Communication*, p. 133; Soper, p. 409; Patrick Wilson, p. 363), although, at the same time, they argue for smaller, more usable collections. This paradox is, of course, rooted in each scholar's need to have, at hand and readily accessible, all of the information that he or she requires and no more. This paradox has been explored extensively by Patrick Wilson (*Public Knowledge*; *Second-Hand Knowledge*).

Garvey and his colleagues at Johns Hopkins have given particular attention to the interactive nature of scholarly investigation. They have concluded that personal interaction is the most fundamental and most important element in scholarly communication. Price has also stressed the importance of such interaction, observing that travel to meet with colleagues and to participate in colloquia has helped the contemporary scholar cope with the proliferation of information (p. 80).

Crane's work remains authoritative on scholars' networks. Among the characteristics that she identifies are: networks are small and highly specialized; participants who are involved in more than one specialty are usually involved in more than one network, and thus provide bridges between networks; due to the exclusivity of networks, they tend to eliminate potentially relevant information from other specialties; only active scholars maintain their participation in networks; younger scholars tend to be excluded from networks; the most established and respected scholars are usually the central figures in networks.

Ten years after publication of Crane's pioneering study, Cronin reviewed the subsequent literature and analyzed its application to information transfer in the social sciences. The importance of networks has been identified for the humanities (Corkill, p. 56;

Smith, p. 6; Frye, p. 12); the social sciences (Brittain, "Pitfalls of User Research," p. 145; Adam, p. 337; Hogeweg-De Haart, p. 13; and Roberts, p. 105); and the sciences (Price; Crane; Garvey). Brittain has noted the particular value of networks in filtering and focusing information (Brittain, *Information and Its Users*, p. 10). Wilson and Farid, in a particularly incisive discussion of scholars' research methods, identified the critical importance of pursuing citation trails (p. 131). Price has noted the contribution that citations make to relating each scholarly work to the total body of scholarship (p. 58). Kuhn has discussed the importance of citations in scholars' information searching practices (p. 428).

Price identified the importance of core journals (pp. 67-69). Citing a British study, Meadows notes that 95 percent of all citations to science journals in the mid–1960s were to only 165 titles out of 2,000 (*Communication in Science*, p. 164). More recent analyses support these findings (Langridge; Neff).

Many analysts have discussed the inequality of scholars' informal information-exchange systems. Price observed that the systems primarily served the most active scholars, whom he estimated to comprise approximately 1 percent of the total scholarly community (p. 44). Subsequent analyses (Frye, p. 134; Meadows, *Communication*, p. 109; Smith, p. 15) have supported his assessment, although they have generally arrived at somewhat higher figures, for example, 5 percent in the social sciences (Brittain, "Information Services," p. 637). Crane noted that networks are dominated by a small core of highly productive scholars (p. 123).

The information-seeking problems of beginning scholars have been discussed by several commentators. The difficulty they encounter in gaining access to information networks (Griffith, p. 134); their dependence on local colleagues, conferences, and library research (Garvey, p. 276; *Scholarly Communication*, p. 91, 134); as well as their sense of isolation (Goslin, p. 37) have been specifically identified.

Various analysts have concluded that even the most active scholars are not entirely well served by their information-seeking practices. Hagstrom has noted that these practices are "often burdensome, inadequate, and lead to additional problems for the larger information system" (p. 124). Crane, Garvey, and the Humanities Information Seminar have discussed at some length the need for active scholars to have more efficient and effective information access.

Garvey has been less than sanguine about technological solutions to scholars' information-seeking problems: "the problem for contemporary scientists is that even if they had perfect [information] retrieval systems they would be presented with so many items that they could not assimilate and process them" (p. 107). The findings of Hiltz, reporting on an experimental electronic information exchange system, would seem to bear this out: use of the system "simply cannot compete in terms of the priorities, with the press of immediate professional demands" (p. 46). Reporting on the results of a different study, McCarroll noted the need for "on-line librarian type services to facilitate the use of the system by members and to develop specific applications" (p. 76).

The information-management problems posed by the so-called "gray literature" are discussed extensively by Garvey, who describes it as the "main concern . . . in the communication structure of science" (p. 64). Price has discussed both the proliferation of specialties and increased travel as means of dealing with information overload.

THE INFLUENCE OF TECHNOLOGY

Technology and Social Change (Allen et al.) is an excellent, extended discussion of this topic, including a number of important and interesting examples of how technological advancements have contributed to important social developments. Harris describes the progress of research libraries and librarians through the manuscript and print eras. *Medieval Scribes, Manuscripts and Libraries* provides interesting recent discussion of these topics by some of the foremost scholars in the field. Eisenstein has thoroughly analyzed the influence of printing on scholarly information. Dizard provides an excellent, basic treatment of the nature and potential impact of the new electronic technology on information, its distribution and use.

FROM COOPERATION TO COLLABORATION

The common responsibility that research librarians share for preserving the record of scholarship has been affirmed in a number of statements in recent years. Gwinn and Mosher have described the holdings of American research libraries as a "national collection held severally" (p. 130), and De Gennaro has described research library collections as a "single, large, distributed collection" (p. 84).

Advocates of these views have, at the same time, attacked the "myth of the self-sufficient collection" (Mosher, p. 21). Mosher (pp. 22-24) has summarized the results of a number of studies of the overlap in research library collections. Although such analysis is still too limited to draw more than the most general conclusions, the data seem to suggest that at least 50 percent of such collections are redundant. Results of a recent survey of research libraries indicate that most have significant uncataloged monograph holdings, ranging from 500 to 159,000 titles, up to 10 percent of individual library collections (Agnew).

Stuart-Stubbs has provided an excellent brief history of resource sharing among research libraries. Martin has observed that, from its inception, interlibrary loan has been treated as a "stepchild" and "not viewed as part of the library's integral structure" (pp. 47-48). A relatively recent study by the Association of Research Libraries notes that "the interlibrary loan future is a struggle to promote increased resource sharing in a climate that enforces concern with recovering expenses" (*Interlibrary Loan in ARL Libraries*). Quite recently, White has observed that "we continue to make [interlibrary loan] appear trivial and unimportant, a sidelight activity to whatever else we do" ("Interlibrary Loan," p. 53). These assessments have been echoed by others (De Gennaro, p. 80; Weber, p. 218; Kronick, p. 134). Govan has discussed the fundamental conflict between preservation and lending, noting that "digitizing text" offers a solution (p. 24). The increasing charges that research libraries are levying for interlibrary lending are identified by Cline.

After reviewing various research library cooperative collection-development programs, Bennett observed: "What emerges from even the most cursory survey of large-scale cooperative collection efforts is the persistence of substantial obstacles" (p. 260). Munn and Dougherty have identified major problems that stand in the way of significant collection development cooperation. Line has noted that, even with advances in resource-sharing activity, research libraries continue to invest heavily in unused material ("Document Delivery," p. 171). Avram has reviewed the difficulties encountered in attempting to create a single national bibliographic database ("Whatever Became").

The sense of competition among research librarians is perhaps best illustrated by the data that the Association of Research Libraries annually publishes, on behalf of and describing its members, the largest research libraries in the United States and Canada. The first table reports collection size. It lists its member libraries in order, according to the size of their collections, and assigns a rank number to each library. It also divides the list into subgroups, according to size. In recent years, these data have been regularly reported and discussed in the *Chronicle of Higher Education.*

Cartter's study of the quality of graduate education, carried out for the American Council on Education in 1966, argued that its "library resources index"—derived from collection size, volumes added annually, and number of current periodical subscriptions—was an essential ingredient in determining institutional quality. Coming, as it did, at the apex of an extended period of university growth, this report exerted an enormous influence on higher education values and perceptions. Not only did it focus on collection size as the determinant of research library quality; it made institutional competition in this area not simply acceptable, but almost mandatory.

Osburn discusses "the enhancement of library prestige through growth" (*Academic Research and Library Resources*, p. 107). De Gennaro notes the efforts invested by research librarians to convince faculty to "equate quantity with quality" in assessing research library collections (p. 181).

Weber has provided an excellent, succinct history of research library cooperation. Rutstein covers major cooperative developments in bibliographic control and resource sharing. Norman D. Stevens' brief history of library networks is useful. Alexander Wilson offers interesting insight into the influence of economic pressures on research library cooperation. Avram identifies major contributions to the rise of networking ("Current Issues in Networking"). Kronick discusses the importance of economic factors in spurring research library cooperation.

It is clear, from discussions of even the most devoted advocates of research library cooperation, just how difficult and demanding those activities are—for example, the costly and intricate procedures developed by the Research Libraries Group for even the very limited collection development cooperation that it has been able to implement (Bennett). The fact that interlibrary loan activity continues to represent approximately 1 percent of total research library circulation (Waldhart, p. 217) suggests the enormity of the problems confronting a major shift from local to general dependency. This is underscored by the small use that scholars make of interlibrary loan (Soper, p. 412; *Scholarly Communication*, p. 133; Meadows, *Communication*, p. 113) as well as the low esteem in which it has been held (DeGennaro, p. 80).

Biggs and Webreck provide excellent summaries and analysis of the efforts to establish a National Periodicals Center. The Arthur D. Little, Inc., study identified the technology problems of the Center proposal. Rowland C. W. Brown and Wetherbee have recently sounded alarms regarding a declining interest in cooperation, as assessed from the national and regional perspectives.

DIRECTING CHANGE

The literature on new information technologies is large and growing rapidly. Vervest has provided a recent informative review of the present and potential use of electronic mail. Hendley discusses CD-ROM and optical publishing. Standera has thoroughly reviewed electronic publishing.

Strawhorn has predicted that the new technology will "encourage an expanded system of informal and semiformal communication that will mimic some of the characteristics of what we know as formal publishing" (p. 23). Gibb foresees the rise of the electronic journal as inevitable, "because the costs of conventional publishing will gradually become unbearable" (p. 51). Reporting on its lack of acceptance in a recent experiment, Senders has nonetheless reconfirmed his conviction that electronic publishing will replace print publication of scholarly journals. Cyert also anticipates that print journal publishing will gradually be replaced by electronic distribution, "although it may be well into the 1990s before this development noticeably affects libraries" (p. 338).

Katzen and Rutimann have described applications of the new technology to scholarly communication in the humanities. King and Kent have discussed such impact in the sciences. Henderson has provided an interesting discussion of "electronic anarchy," due to uncontrolled and unorganized scholarly publication in electronic form.

It is difficult to characterize accurately the total sweep of reactions on the part of research librarians, and others closely interested in research libraries, to the new technology. All agree that the library will change, probably substantially. Some (De Gennaro; Moran; Rochell) deal with the change within the context of present practice, thus emphasizing continuity. Others (Adams; Battin, "The Electronic Library"; Gurnsey; Hyatt; Matheson; Sack) emphasize differences, but without explicitly abandoning much that has and continues to characterize the research library.

McCoy identified expectations related to development of a scholar's workstation. Battin ("The Library"), Cimbala, Molholt, and Neff have discussed, from a variety of perspectives, the prospects of combining the research library with other campus information services.

A number of commentators, including Bell (*The Coming of Post–Industrial Society*), James Martin, and Toffler, predict a radically altered electronic future in which enormous quantities of information in this form will be readily available, from a wide variety of sources, to anyone with a personal computer. Recognizing the enormous problem involved in organizing this information, Bell has observed that everyone will have to "create his own index" (*Winding Passage*, p. 58).

It is Ziman who has noted that, for the scholar, "'catching up with the literature' seems an unending labor whose product may be no more than a dusty pile of unused journals and reprints on the office desk" (p. 102). Foskett has observed:

> There is no point in piling more and bigger computer-produced bibliographic masterpieces on the laps or desks of people who seek help precisely because they are weighed down with the mass of information they already have, and cannot see the pattern for the multiplicity of threads (*Information Service in Libraries*, p. 80).

Patrick Wilson has noted that: "a computer-based file of unevaluated bits of data may be said to constitute a data bank, but it is no information center. Critical analysis and synthesis are the crucial ingredients" (*Public Knowledge*, p. 30).

Lancaster is certainly the most widely known and respected library futurist. He predicts a future in which "the library and its collection and catalog become deinstitutionalized or . . . disembodied" (*Libraries and Librarians*, p. 144). Indeed, he suggests that the library may be "bypassed by a number of users [because] simplified search procedures allow these persons a comfortable level of access to a wide variety of data bases and data banks, to the question-answering file built up by the libraries, and to an increasingly diverse array of resources in full text form" (p. 147). Looking ahead to a "paperless society," Lancaster challenges librarians to define their future role, suggesting that, unless the profession "now faces up to the question 'Whither libraries?' it will indeed face the prospect of 'wither libraries'" ("Whither Libraries?", p. 357).

The literature on organizational change is enormous and continuing to grow. An excellent recent discussion is provided by Connor and Lake. Still the most extensive and thoughtful treatment of change in librarianship is Wasserman. Many of the other works cited in this essay make interesting observations on this important and complex topic. For example, Hyatt and Santiago have noted:

> Given [present] conditions, are librarians in a position to effect change? Librarians who wish to maintain a tradition of the library as a collection of printed material and who strive to increase such collections will have little impact. However, librarians who perceive the library as an information center and who seek to provide services at the convenience of their users can enhance the library's role in the academic and research activities of their institutions (pp. 9-10).

Probably the best treatment of the role and responsibilities of the university press is Kerr. Meyer and Philabaum have discussed the financial difficulties of scholarly publishing. Ward has identified scholars' concerns regarding financial influences on scholarly publishers' editorial judgments. Loumer has expressed concern about increasing amounts of scholarly information in electronic form bypassing established publication and review channels.

The dynamics of the modern university, including those governing change, are discussed, from different perspectives, by William R. Brown, Corson, Millett, and Logan Wilson.

CONTROLLED COMPLETENESS: CONSOLIDATING THE RECORD OF SCHOLARSHIP

Garvey has discussed at length the problems created by the unrefereed and uncontrolled elements of the literature of scholarship.

Ziman has identified the fundamental importance to scholarship of the referee system: "An article in a reputable journal ... bears the *imprimatur* of scientific authenticity, as given to it by the editor and the referees whom he may have consulted" (p. 111). Merton and Zukerman have analyzed the workings of this system. Osburn has described its fundamental importance with respect to the scholarly journal ("The Place of the Journal"). Geiger has discussed the difficulties of maintaining this practice effectively in an unstructured electronic information environment.

The particular problems of government publications are dealt with by Hernon and McClure. *Preservation of Library Materials* provides an excellent recent survey of preservation issues and practices. "Optical Scanning" reviews relatively recent developments with this extremely important technology. Stanton, et. al., discuss the capabilities of a number of different scanning devices.

RELIABLE CONVENIENCE: THE FUTURE RESEARCH LIBRARY

In recent years, a number of analysts have stressed the subjective nature of information seeking. Drawing upon communications research, Dervin has identified its "situational" character:

> Meanings are in people. No message means the same thing to different people. No situation is seen the same by different people. The same message read on two different days will not mean the same thing to the same person. The same person in the 'same' situation on two different days will not see that situation the same way (p. 27).

Streatfield describes the "forlorn search for a one-to-one coincidence between information products and expressed needs for information" (p. 225). Rouse and Rouse have stressed the need for flexibility: "Because information needs change in time and depend on the particular information seeker, systems should be sufficiently flexible to allow the user to adapt the information seeking process to his own current needs" (p. 135). Neill, in an effort to reconcile these views with the need to organize and structure information, concluded:

The history of the development of intellectual access to the store of knowledge is a history of the tension between the fluid uniqueness of the individual inquirer and the essential stability and concreteness of the store of knowledge itself.... As Cutter noted, it is a difficulty in the nature of things. Information does exist "out there" and we must deal with it from "in here" (p. 208).

All of these commentators have stressed the fundamental importance of interaction between information seeker and information provider.

The difficulties and shortcomings of language in the information-transfer process have been reviewed by Bar-Hillel. Gumperz has analyzed the linguistic differences among social groups. Labon discusses the social settings of linguistic change. Hertzler provides an excellent review of findings related to the varied languages of scholarship. Dirckx has examined the language of medicine in detail.

Patrick Wilson has noted the efforts of catalogers to keep pace with the changes in disciplinary vocabularies ("The Catalog as Access," pp. 11-12). Wilberly has discussed the problems involved in utilizing a field's vocabulary in subject cataloging. Needham has identified the need for a unique index language: "The adequate representation of subjects in a retrieval system cannot rely solely on the use of common language. Modifications of both vocabulary and syntax are required; a controlled language, i.e., an index language, has to be created" (p. 240). Lancaster has noted that: "the index language exists primarily to bring the vocabulary of the indexer and the vocabulary of the searcher into coincidence" (*Vocabulary Control*, p. 2). Foskett provides an excellent overall discussion of subject analysis. Classification and indexing in the Social Sciences (Foskett), Science (Vickery), and Humanities (Langridge) have been separately analyzed.

Line has discussed the added capabilities of bibliographic systems that can be managed and interpreted by information experts for the benefit of the information seeker:

If . . . one could assume an intermediary always between the information and the user, information systems could be developed to almost any level of complexity; the enormous constraint of ready usability would cease to exist, and this should make possible for far more efficient and effective information retrieval systems to be developed ("The Information Uses," p. 426).

The image of the librarian as therapist is drawn from Patrick Wilson:

Perhaps we should envision, as the proper aim of bibliographical policy, the creation of arrangements by which the perhaps unfelt needs of scientific workers and the general public would be diagnosed by teams of bibliographical therapists, who would satisfy those needs with suitable doses of literature. How else can we expect that the existing stock of writings will be fully utilized? (*Two Kinds of Power*, p. 144).

Wyer's 1930 discussion of reference work illustrates the reactive posture then in vogue. A recent text on university library reference service advocates an essentially reactive posture (Stevens and Smith). The distinction between reactive and active reference service has been made, although perhaps not in these terms, by a variety of commentators (Foskett, *Pathways*; *Special Librarianship*; Rothstein; White, "The Role of Reference").

Cognitive authority and its application to librarianship is discussed by Patrick Wilson (*Second–Hand Knowledge*). The value of personal interaction between librarian and client in an information-delivery environment has been extensively analyzed by Neway.

REFERENCES

Adam, Ralph. "Can the Transmission of Sociological Knowledge Be Made More Effective?" *International Social Science Journal* 34 (1982): 329-45.

Adams, Roy J. *Information Technology and Libraries: A Future for Academic Libraries.* London: Croom Helm, 1986.

Agnew, Grace; Landram, Christina; and Richards, Jane. "Monograph Arrearages in Research Libraries." *Library Resources and Technical Services* 29 (October 1985): 343-59.

Allen, Francis R.; Hart, Hornell; Miller, Dalbert C.; Ogburn, William F.; and Nimkoff, Meyer F. *Technology and Social Change.* New York: Appleton-Century-Crofts, 1957.

Avram, Henriette D. "Current Issues in Networking." *The Journal of Academic Librarianship* 12 (September 1986): 205-9.

———. "Whatever Became of a National Database?" *Library Quarterly* 53 (July 1983): 269-78.

Bar-Hillel, Yehoshua. *Language and Information.* Reading, Mass.: Addison-Wesley, 1964.

Battin, Patricia. "The Electronic Library—A Vision for the Future." *EDUCOM Bulletin* 19 (Summer 1984): 1-7.

———. "The Library: Center of the Restructured University." *College and Research Libraries* 45 (May 1984): 170-77.

———. "Preservation: Proposal for a National Approach." Paper presented at the 6th Annual Conference of Directors of Research Libraries in OCLC, 1988. Unpublished.

Bebout, Lois; Davis, Donald, Jr.; and Oehlerts, Donald. "User Studies in the Humanities: A Survey and a Proposal." *RQ* 15 (Fall 1975): 40-44.

Bell, Daniel. *The Coming of Post-Industrial Society.* New York: Basic Books, 1973.

———. *Winding Passage.* Cambridge, Mass.: Abt Books, 1980.

Bennett, Scott. "Current Initiatives and Issues in Collection Management." *The Journal of Academic Librarianship* 10 (November 1984): 257-61.

Biggs, Mary. "The Proposed National Periodicals Center 1973-1980: Study, Dissension, and Retreat." *Resource Sharing and Information Networks* 1 (Spring/Summer 1984): 1-22.

Breton, Ernest J. "Why Engineers Don't Use Databases." *ASIS Bulletin* 7 (August 1981): 20-23.

Brittain, J. Michael. "Information Services and Knowledge Creation in the Social Sciences." *International Social Science Journal* 38 (1986): 631-41.

———. *Information and Its Users: A Review with Special Reference to the Social Sciences.* Bath, Eng.: Bath University Press, 1970.

———. "Pitfalls of User Research and Some Neglected Areas." *Social Science Information Studies* 2 (1982): 139-48.

———. "Relevance of Social Science Output Worldwide." *International Social Science Journal* 37 (1985): 259-75.

Brown, Rowland C. W. "The Nationwide Network and OCLC: A Vision and a Role." In *Toward a Common Vision of Library Networking: Proceedings of the Library of Congress Network Advisory Committee Meeting, December 9-11, 1985*. Washington, D.C.: Library of Congress, 1986.

Brown, William R. *Academic Politics*. University, Ala.: University of Alabama Press, 1982.

Bunge, Charles A. "A Brief Overview of the Development of Reference Services in American Libraries." In *Reference Service: A Perspective*, edited by Sul H. Lee. Ann Arbor: Pierian Press, 1983.

Cartter, Allan M. *An Assessment of Quality in Graduate Education*. Washington, D.C.: American Council on Education, 1966.

Cimbala, Diane J. "The Scholarly Information Center: An Organizational Model." *College and Research Libraries* 48 (September 1987): 393-98.

Cline, Gloria S. "The High Price of Interlibrary Loan Service." *RQ* 27 (Fall 1987): 80-86.

Connor, Patrick, and Lake, Linda K. *Managing Organizational Change*. New York: Praeger, 1988.

Corkill, Cynthia, and Mann, Margaret. *Information Needs in the Humanities: Two Postal Surveys*. Sheffield, Eng.: University of Sheffield, 1987.

Corson, John J. *Governance of Colleges and Universities*. New York: McGraw-Hill, 1960.

Crane, Diana. *Invisible Colleges*. Chicago: The University of Chicago Press, 1972.

Cronin, Blaise. "Invisible Colleges and Information Transfer: A Review and Commentary with Particular Reference to the Social Sciences." *Journal of Documentation* 38 (September 1982): 212-36.

Cyert, Richard M. "Distributed Computer Systems and Electronic Publishing in Education." In *Electronic Publishing Plus*, edited by Martin Greenberger. White Plains, N.Y.: Knowledge Industry Publications, 1985.

Davison, Keith. *Theory of Classification*. London: Clive Bingley, 1966.

DeGennaro, Richard. *Libraries, Technology, and the Information Marketplace*. Boston: G. K. Hall, 1987.

Dervin, Brenda. "Useful Theory for Librarianship: Communication, Not Information." *Drexel Library Quarterly* 13 (July 1977): 16-32.

Dewey Decimal Classification and Relative Index. Edition 20, edited by John P. Comaromi. Albany, N.Y.: Forest Press, 1989.

Dirckx, John H. *The Language of Medicine*. 2d ed. New York: Praeger, 1983.

Dizard, Wilson P. *The Coming Information Age: An Overview of Technology, Economics, and Politics.* New York: Longman, 1982.

Dougherty, Richard M. "Research Libraries in an International Setting: Requirements for Expanded Resource Sharing." *College and Research Libraries* 46 (September 1985): 383-89.

Eisenstein, Elizabeth L. *The Printing Press as an Agent of Change: Communications and Cultural Transformation in Early-Modern Europe.* Cambridge, Eng.: Cambridge University Press, 1979.

Foskett, A. C. *Subject Approach to Information.* 4th ed. London: Clive Bingley, 1982.

Foskett, D. J. *Classification and Indexing in the Social Sciences.* 2d ed. London: Butterworths, 1974.

———. *Information Service in Libraries.* London: Crosby Lockwood, 1958.

———. *Pathways for Communication: Books and Libraries in the Information Age.* London: Clive Bingley, 1984.

Frye, Northrup. "The Search for Acceptable Words." *Daedalus* 102 (Spring 1973): 11-26.

Garvey, William D. *Communication: The Essence of Science.* Oxford, Eng.: Pergamon Press, 1979.

Geiger, Stephen R. "Electronics in Publishing and the Consequences." *Scholarly Publishing* 18 (October 1986): 29-32.

Gibb, John Michael. "Information Transfer in Europe." In *Trends in Information Transfer*, edited by Philip Hills. Westport, Conn.: Greenwood Press, 1982.

Goslin, David A. "Topology of Information and Vehicles of Communication." *International Social Science Journal* 26 (1974): 427-37.

Govan, J. F. "Preservation and Resource Sharing: Conflicting or Complimentary?" *IFLA Journal* 12 (1986): 20-24.

Griffith, Belvar C., and Miller, James A. "Networks of Informal Communication Among Scientifically Productive Scientists." In *Communication Among Scientists and Engineers*, edited by Carnot E. Nelson and Donald K. Pollock. Lexington, Mass.: Heath, 1970.

Guest, Susan S. "The Use of Bibliographic Tools by Humanities Faculty at the State University of New York at Albany." *Reference Librarian* 18 (Summer 1987): 157-72.

Gumperz, John J. *Language in Social Groups.* Stanford: Stanford University Press, 1971.

Gurnsey, John. *The Information Professions in the Electronic Age.* London: Clive Bingley, 1985.

Gwinn, Nancy E., and Mosher, Paul H. "Coordinating Collection Development: The RLG Conspectus." *College and Research Libraries* 44 (March 1983): 128-40.

Hagstrom, Warren O. "Factors Related to the Use of Different Modes of Publishing Research in Four Scientific Fields." In *Communication Among Scientists and Engineers*, edited by Carnot E. Nelson and Donald K. Pollock. Lexington, Mass.: Heath, 1970.

Halvorson, Homer. "The Reference Function in the University and Research Library." In *The Reference Function in the Library*, edited by Pierce Butler. Chicago: University of Chicago Press, 1943.

Harris, Michael H. *History of Libraries in the Western World*. Metuchen, N.J.: Scarecrow Press, 1984.

Henderson, Helen. "Will There Be Electronic Anarchy?" In *New Trends in Electronic Publishing and Electronic Libraries; Essen Symposium*, edited by Ahmed H. Helal and Joachim W. Weiss. Essen, Ger.: Essen University Library, 1984.

Hendley, Tony. *CD-ROM and Optical Publishing Systems*. Westport, Conn.: Meckler, 1987.

Hernon, Peter, and McClure, Charles R. *Federal Information Policies in the 1980s: Conflicts and Issues*. Norwood, N.J.: Ablex Publishing Corporation, 1987.

Hertzler, Joyce O. *A Sociology of Language*. New York: Random House, 1965.

Hiltz, Starr Roxanne. "An Overview of the Nature, Purpose and Initial Findings." In *Electronic Communication: Technology and Impacts*, edited by Madeline M. Henderson and Marcia J. MacNaughton. Washington, D.C.: American Association for the Advancement of Science, 1980.

Hogeweg-De Haart, H. P. "Social Science and the Characteristics of Social Science Information and Its Users." *International Forum of Information and Documentation* 8 (January 15, 1983): 99-125.

Humanities Information Research: Proceedings of a Seminar; Sheffield 1980, edited by Sue Stone. Sheffield, Eng.: University of Sheffield, Center for Research on User Studies, 1980.

Hyatt, James A., and Santiago, Aurora A. *University Libraries in Transition*. Washington, D.C.: National Association of College and University Business Officers, 1987.

Interlibrary Loan in ARL Libraries. Washington, D.C.: Association of Research Libraries, 1986.

Jones, Clyve; Chapman, Michael; and Woods, Pamela Carr. "The Characteristics of the Literature Used by Historians." *Journal of Librarianship* 4 (July 1972): 137-56.

Katzen, M., and Howley, S. M. *Recent Initiatives in Communications in the Humanities*. Boston Spa: British Library Lending Division, 1984.

Katzen, May. "Electronic Publishing in the Humanities." *Scholarly Publishing* 18 (October 1986): 5-16.

———. "A National Information Network." *Scholarly Publishing* 19 (July 1988): 210-16.

Kent, A. K. "Scientific and Technical Publishing in the 1980s." In *The Future of the Printed Word: The Impact and the Implications of the New Communications Technology*, edited by Philip Hills. Westport, Conn.: Greenwood Press, 1980.

Kerr, Chester. *A Report on American University Presses*. Chapel Hill, N.C.: The University of North Carolina Press, 1949.

———. "The Kerr Report Revisited." *Scholarly Publishing* 1 (October 1969): 5-30.

Kilgour, Frederick G. *Beyond Bibliography*. London: The British Library, 1985.

King, Donald W. "Electronic Alternatives to Paper-Based Publishing in Science and Technology." In *The Future of the Printed Word: The Impact and the Implications of the New Communications Technology*, edited by Philip Hills. Westport, Conn.: Greenwood Press, 1980.

Kronick, David A. "Goodbye to Farewells—Resource Sharing and Cost Sharing." *The Journal of Academic Librarianship* 36 (July 1982): 132-36.

Kuhn, Thomas S. *The Structure of Scientific Revolutions*. 2d ed. Chicago: University of Chicago Press, 1970.

Labon, William. *Sociolinguistic Patterns*. Philadelphia: University of Pennsylvania Press, 1972.

Lancaster, F. W. *Libraries and Librarians in an Age of Electronics*. Arlington, Va.: Information Resources Press, 1982.

———. *Vocabulary Control for Information Retrieval*. Washington, D.C.: Information Resources Press, 1972.

———. "Whither Libraries? or Wither Libraries." *College and Research Libraries* 39 (September 1978): 345-57.

Langridge, D. W. *Classification and Indexing in the Humanities*. London: Butterworths, 1976.

Line, Maurice B. "Document Delivery, Now and in the Future." *ASLIB Proceedings* 23 (April 1983): 167-76.

———. "The Information Uses and Needs of Social Scientists: An Overview of INFROSS." *ASLIB Proceedings* 23 (August 1971): 412-33.

———. *Towards the Improvement of Social Science Information Systems: Overview of Research Carried Out 1971-75*. Bath, Eng.: Bath University, 1980.

Little, Arthur D., Inc. *A Comparative Evaluation of Alternative Systems for the Provision of Effective Access to Periodical Literature*. Washington, D.C.: The National Commission on Libraries and Information Science, 1979.

Loumer, Rowland. "Implications of the New Technologies of Information." *Scholarly Publishing* 16 (April 1985): 197-210.

Lubetsky, Seymour. "Ideology of Bibliographic Cataloging: Progress and Retrogression." In *The Nature and Future of the Catalog: Proceedings of the ALA's Information Science and Automation Division's 1975 and*

1977 Institutes on the Catalog, edited by Maurice J. Freedman and S. Michael Malinconico. Phoenix: Oryx Press, 1979.

McCarrol, Jane H. "EIES for a Community Involved in R & D of Devices for the Disabled." In *Electronic Communication: Technology and Impacts*, edited by Madeline M. Henderson and Marcia J. MacNaughton. Washington, D.C.: American Association for the Advancement of Science, 1980.

McClure, Charles B. "A Reference Theory of Specific Information Retrieval." *RQ* 13 (Fall 1973): 207-12.

McCoy, Richard W. "The Electronic Scholar: Essential Tasks for the Scholarly Community." *Library Journal* 110 (October 1, 1985): 39-42.

Martin, James. *The Wired Society*. Englewood Cliffs, N.J.: Prentice-Hall, 1978.

Martin, Susan K. "The Impact of Technology on Interlibrary Lending." *Interlending and Document Supply* 12 (April 1984): 47-51.

Masuda, Yoneji. *The Information Society as Post-Industrial Society*. Washington, D.C.: World Future Society, 1980.

Matheson, Nina W. "The Academic Library Nexus." *College and Research Libraries* 45 (May 1984): 207-13.

Meadows, A. J. *Communication in Science*. London: Butterworths, 1974.

———. "The Future of the Printed Word: Economic and Social Factors." In *The Future of the Printed Word: The Impact and Implications of the New Communications Technology*. Westport, Conn.: Greenwood Press, 1980.

———. *New Technology and Developments in the Communication of Research during the 1980s*. Leicester, Eng.: University of Leicester, 1980.

Medieval Scribes, Manuscripts, and Libraries, edited by M. B. Parkes and Andrew W. Watson. London: Scolar Press, 1978.

Merton, Ralph K., and Zukerman, Harriet. "Patterns of Evaluation in Science: Institutionalization, Structure and Functions of the Referee System." *Minerva* 9 (January 1971): 66-100.

Meyer, Sheldon, and Philabaum, Leslie E. "What is a University Press?" *Scholarly Publishing* 11 (April 1980): 213-19.

Meyriat, Jean. "Use of Information in Science and Research: Social Sciences." *International Forum of Information and Documentation* 9 (July 1984): 10-12.

Millett, John D. *Decision Making and Administration in Higher Education*. Kent, Ohio: Kent State University Press, 1968.

Molholt, Pat. "On Converging Paths: The Computing Center and the Library." *Journal of Academic Librarianship* 11 (November 1985): 284-88.

Moran, Barbara B. *Academic Libraries: The Changing Knowledge Centers of Colleges and Universities*. Washington, D.C.: Association for the Study of Higher Education, 1984.

Morrison, Perry D. "Since Bath: A Review of Published Information Transfer Studies in the Social and Behavioral Sciences, 1974-1978." *Behavioral and Social Sciences Librarian* 1 (Fall 1979): 1-22.

Mosher, Paul H. "A National Scheme for Collaboration in Collection Development." In *Coordinating Cooperative Collection Development* edited by Wilson Luquire. New York: Haworth Press, 1986.

Munn, Robert F. "Cooperation Will Not Save Us." *The Journal of Academic Librarianship* 12 (July 1985): 166-67.

Needham, C. H. *Organizing Knowledge in Libraries*. 2d ed. London: Andre Deutsch, 1971.

Neill, S. D. "The Dilemma of the Subjective in Information Organization and Retrieval." *The Journal of Documentation* 43 (September 1987): 193-211.

Neff, Raymond K. "Merging Libraries and Computer Centers: Manifest Destiny or Manifestly Deranged? An Academic Services Perspective." *EDUCOM Bulletin* 20 (Winter 1985): 8-12, 16.

Neway, Julie M. *The Information Specialist as a Team Player in the Research Process*. Westport, Conn.: Greenwood Press, 1985.

Nielsen, Brian. "Teacher or Intermediary: Alternative Professional Models in the Information Age." *College and Research Libraries* 43 (May 1982): 183-91.

"Optical Scanning: How it Helps, How it Works, and What it Costs." *Scholarly Communication* 2 (Fall 1985): 1-2.

Osburn, Charles B. *Academic Research and Library Resources: Changing Patterns in America*. Westport, Conn.: Greenwood Press, 1979.

―――. "The Place of the Journal in the Scholarly Communications System." *Library Resources and Technical Services* 28 (October/December 1984): 315-24.

Preservation of Library Materials, edited by Merrily A. Smith. 2 volumes. Munich: K. G. Saur, 1987.

Price, Derek J. De Solla. *Little Science, Big Science . . . And Beyond*. New York: Columbia University Press, 1986.

Roberts, Stephen A. "The Management and Development of Information and Library Provision in the Social Sciences." *Journal of Documentation* 40 (June 1984): 94-119.

―――, and Brittain, J. Michael. "Demand and Supply Patterns for Documents and Data in the United Kingdom." *International Social Science Journal* 33 (1981): 50-71.

Rochell, Carlton C. "The Next Decade: Distributed Access to Information." *Library Journal* 112 (February 1, 1987): 42-48.

Rogers, Rutherford D. "The Western Information Society." In *New Information Technologies and Libraries*, edited by H. Liebaers, W. J. Haas, and W. E. Biervliet. Dordrecht, Hollard: D. Reidel, 1985.

Rogers, Rutherford D., and Weber, David C. *University Library Administration.* New York: H. W. Wilson Company, 1971.

Rothstein, Samuel. "Reference Service: The New Dimension in Librarianship." *College and Research Libraries* 22 (January 1961): 11-18.

Rouse, William B., and Rouse, Sandra H. "Human Information Seeking and Design of Information Systems." *Information Processing and Management* 20 (1984): 129-38.

Rutimann, Hans. "The MLA and the Computer." *Scholarly Publishing* 19 (October 1978): 18-23.

Rutstein, Joel S. "National and Local Resource Sharing: Issues in Cooperative Collection Development." *Collection Management* 7 (Summer 1985): 1-16.

Sack, John S. "Open Systems for Open Minds: Building the Library without Walls." *College and Research Libraries* 47 (November 1986): 535-44.

Schiller, Anita R. "Reference Service: Instruction or Information." *Library Quarterly* 35 (January 1965): 52-60.

Scholarly Communication: The Report of the National Enquiry. Baltimore, Md.: Johns Hopkins University Press, 1979.

Seal, Robert A. "Academic Branch Libraries." *Advances in Librarianship* 14 (1986): 175-210.

Senders, John W. "I Have Seen the Future and It Doesn't Work: The Electronic Journal Experiment." In *Scholarly Publishing in an Era of Change.* Washington, D.C.: Society for Scholarly Publishing, 1981.

Smith, D. B. *Information Problems in the Humanities: A Report on the British Library Seminar.* Boston Spa: The British Library, 1975.

The Social Sciences: The Supply of and Demand for Documentation and Data, a Report to UNESCO, edited by J. Michael Brittain. London: Rossendale, 1982.

Soper, Mary Ellen. "Characteristics and Use of Personal Collections." *Library Quarterly* 46 (October 1976): 397-415.

Special Librarianship: A New Reader, edited by Eugene B. Jackson. Metuchen, N.J.: Scarecrow Press, 1980.

Stanton, Tom; Burns, Diane; and Venit, S. "Page-to-Disk Technology: Nine State-of-the-Art Scanners." *PC Magazine* (September 30, 1986): 129-77.

Standera, Olrich. *The Electronic Era of Publishing.* New York: Elsevier, 1987.

Stenstrom, Patricia, and McBride, Ruth B. "Serial Use by Social Science Faculty: A Survey." *College and Research Libraries* 44 (July 1983): 426-31.

Stevens, Norman D. "Library Networks and Resource Sharing in the United States: An Historical and Philosophical Overview." *Journal of the American Society for Information Science* 31 (November 1980): 406-12.

Stevens, Rolland E. "A Study of Interlibrary Loan." *College and Research Libraries* 35 (September 1974): 336-43.
―――, and Smith, Linda C. *Reference Work in the University Library.* Littleton, Colo.: Libraries Unlimited, 1986.
Stieg, Margaret F. "The Information Needs of Historians." *College and Research Libraries* 42 (November 1981): 549-60.
Stone, Sue. "Humanities Scholars: Information Needs and Uses." *Journal of Documentation* 38 (December 1982): 292-313.
Strawhorn, John M. "Future Methods and Techniques." In *The Future of the Printed Word: The Impact and Implications of the New Communications Technology*, edited by Philip Hills. Westport, Conn.: Greenwood Press, 1980.
Streatfield, D. "Moving Towards the Information User: Some Research and Its Implications." *Social Science Information Studies* 3 (1983): 223-40.
Stuart-Stubbs, Basil. "An Historical Look at Resource Sharing." *Library Trends* 23 (April 1975): 649-64.
Thompson, James. *The End of Libraries.* London: Clive Bingley, 1982.
Toffler, Alvin. *The Third Wave.* New York: Morrow, 1980.
The Use of Library Materials: The Pittsburgh Study, edited by Allen Kent, et al. New York: Marcel Dekker, 1979.
Vervest, Peter. *Electronic Mail and Message Handling.* Westport, Conn.: Quorum Books, 1985.
Vickery, B. C. *Classification and Indexing in Science.* 3d ed. London: Butterworths, 1975.
Waldhart, Thomas J. "Patterns of Interlibrary Loan Among ARL University Libraries." *Library and Information Science Research* 7 (July 1985): 209-29.
Ward, John William. "How Scholars Regard University Presses." *Scholarly Publishing* 17 (April 1986): 255-67.
Wasserman, Paul. *The New Librarianship: A Challenge for Change.* New York: R. R. Bowker, 1972.
Weber, David C. "A Century of Cooperative Programs Among Academic Libraries." *College and Research Libraries* 37 (May 1976): 205-21.
Webreck, Susan J. "National Periodicals Center." *Encyclopedia of Library and Information Science* 40 (1986): 321-38.
Weintraub, Karl J. "The Humanistic Scholar and the Library." *Library Quarterly* 50 (January 1980): 22-39.
Wetherbee, Louella V. "Remarks on the Role of Regional Networks in National Networking." In *Toward a Common Vision in Library Networking: Proceedings of the Library of Congress Network Advisory Committee Meeting, December 9-11, 1985.* Washington, D.C.: Library of Congress, 1986.

White, Herbert S. "The Role of Reference Service in the Mission of the Academic Library." In *Reference Service: A Perspective*, edited by Sul H. Lee. Ann Arbor: Pierian Press, 1983.
───. "Interlibrary Loan: An Old Idea in a New Setting." *Library Journal* 112 (July 1987): 53-54.
Wilberly, Jr., Stephen E. "Subject Access in the Humanities and the Precision of the Humanist's Vocabulary." *Library Quarterly* 53 (October 1983): 420-33.
Wilson, Alexander. "Collections Development and Services in Recession." *IFLA Journal* 9 (1983):11-19.
Wilson, Kathryn B. "The Impact of User Frustration on Humanities Research." *College and Research Libraries* 42 (July 1981): 361-65.
Wilson, Logan. *American Academics*. New York: Oxford University Press, 1979.
Wilson, Patrick. "The Catalog as Access Mechanism: Background and Concepts." *Library Resources and Technical Services* 27 (January-March 1983): 361-65.
───. *Public Knowledge, Private Ignorance; Toward a Library and Information Policy*. Westport, Conn.: Greenwood Press, 1977.
───. *Second-Hand Knowledge: An Inquiry into Cognitive Authority*. Westport, Conn.: Greenwood Press, 1983.
───. *Two Kinds of Power: An Essay on Bibliographical Control*. Berkeley: University of California Press, 1968.
───, and Farid, Mona. "On the Use of the Records of Research." *Library Quarterly* 49 (April 1979): 127-45.
Wilson, Pauline. *Stereotype and Status: Librarians in the United States*. Westport, Conn.: Greenwood Press, 1982.
Wyer, James I. *Reference Work*. Chicago: American Library Association, 1930.
Zaleznik, Abraham. "Management of Disappointment." In *Executive Success: Making It in Management*, edited by E. Collins. New York: John Wiley, 1983.
Ziman, J. M. *Public Knowledge: An Essay Concerning the Social Dimension of Science*. Cambridge, Eng.: Cambridge University Press, 1968.

Index

Advanced scholars, 25-27

Beginning scholars, 20, 25-26
Bibliographic apparatus, 8-9, 11-12, 36-38, 68; consolidated, 39, 63, 67-68, 75; distinctive vocabulary, 82; electronic, 39, 67-68, 73-75, 79; incompleteness, 45; two-tiered structure, 11-12, 39, 73; use by scholars, 21-24
Branch libraries, 10
British Library Lending Division, 49-52
Browsing, 24, 26

Carrels, 24
Cataloging systems, 8, 37, 46, 73
CD-ROM, 58
Center for Research Libraries, 47-48, 51
Circulation of library materials, 10
Citation searching, 25-26
Classification schemes, 8, 37, 46
Collections. *See* Research library collections
Conference proceedings, 69
Copyists, 32-33, 36
Core literature, 21-22

Electronic era, 31, 34-35, 38-40, 57-59, 69
Electronic mail, 84
Electronic publication, 58

Facsimile transmission, 58
Farmington Plan, 47-48, 51
Futurists, 59-60

Government publications, 58, 70
Gray literature, 38, 69

Inactive scholars, 20, 26-27
Indexes, 67-68, 73-74; terminology, 68, 80-81
Information overload, 23, 27, 60-61
Information technology, 31, 51, 54, 57-58
Interlibrary loan, 44, 47

Library hours, 10
Library instruction, 13-14
Library of Congress, 47, 51
Library of record, 47, 51

Manuscript era, 31-33
MARC database, 47-48, 51
Microfilm preservation, 71-72

National Periodicals Center, 43, 49-54
National Program for Acquisition and Cataloging, 51
National Union Catalog, 47

OCLC (Online Computer Library Center), 47-48, 51
Online bibliographic databases, 58
Online catalogs, 58

PL-480, 48
Print era, 31, 33-34

Record of scholarship, 7-8, 31; beginning of, 32; center for, 67, 76, 83-84; centralized, 67, 75-76; completeness, 43, 63, 67, 75-76; complexity, 34, 74; consolidated, 39, 67, 75-76; core materials, 45, 52, 68; electronic, 38-39, 61-63, 67-70, 79; exponential growth, 28; responsibility of research librarians, 7-8, 14, 25, 83
Referees, 23, 33-34, 61, 69-70
Reference service, 13-15, 38; active, 83; interactive, 83-84; reactive, 83; self-service, 13-15, 84; use by scholars, 22-23
Research librarians: and change, 57, 64; cognitive authority, 84; collaboration among, 43, 51, 53, 61; competition among, 43, 45-46, 52-53; conflict between preservation and use, 9-11, 15, 84; diagnostic skills, 83; expertness, 13-14; interest in systematization, 9; as intermediaries, 79, 82-85; leadership role, 54, 61, 64; quest for completeness, 7-8, 15, 67, 76; quest for control, 7, 9-10, 15, 67, 76; stereotypes, 10

Research librarians' role, 7-8, 35, 43, 63, 83; electronic era, 39; manuscript era, 35-36; print era, 36
Research libraries: complexity of, 12-13, 24, 37-38; as information centers, 60-61, 79, 85; as museums, 59; value to scholars, 23
Research library collections: access, 35-37, 72; incompleteness, 7-8, 36, 43-44; redundant holdings, 36, 43, 45, 53-54; unique holdings, 44; use by scholars, 21-22; use by visiting scholars, 44
Research reports, 69
Reviewers. *See* Referees
RLG (Research Libraries Group), 47-48, 51
RLIN (Research Libraries Information Network), 47

Scholarly publishers, 61-63
Scholarly record. *See* Record of scholarship
Scholars: consumers of scholarly information, 19-20; information-seeking methods, 25-27; need for convenience, 19-21, 27-28, 60, 82, 84-85; need for reliability, 19-20, 28, 82, 84-85; producers of scholarly information, 19-20; research methods, 22, 25-28; specialization, 28; travel, 28; use of research libraries, 21-25
Scholars' networks, 25
Shared cataloging, 47
Students, 13-14, 26

Terminology. *See* Vocabularies

USBE (United States Book Exchange), 48

Vocabularies: common, 80-81; distinctive, 80-81; of librarians, 81-82; of scholarly disciplines, 80-81

ABOUT THE AUTHOR

ELDRED SMITH is a Professor at the University of Minnesota. He has served as University Librarian/Director of Libraries at the University of Minnesota, the State University of New York at Buffalo, and the University of California at Berkeley. His articles have appeared in *College and Research Libraries*, *The Library Journal*, *The Canadian Library Journal*, as well as other journals, symposia, and anthologies.

DATE DUE

324514